About the Author

Diego Pizano was born in Bogotá, Colombia. He studied economics at the Universidad de los Andes in Bogotá and the University of Cambridge in England. Between 1982 and 1986 he was the economic advisor to the President of Colombia. He has been a consultant to the Inter-American Development Bank, the World Bank, and a researcher for Fedesarrollo, a think tank in Bogotá and for the "Institut für Iberoamerika-kunde" in Hamburg. For more than twenty-five years he was the economic and international advisor for the Colombian Coffee Federation, and he represented his country at the International Coffee Organization in London. He served as Plenipotentiary Minister at the Colombian Embassy in Washington. He has been a lecturer at the Universidad de los Andes (Bogotá), where he is Vice Chairman of the Board of Directors. He is affiliated as an external faculty member at the Center of Latin American Studies at Vanderbilt University (USA) and is the President of the Association of the Common Code for the Coffee Community based in Bonn, Germany. He has published several works including: *Grupo Andino: Objetivos, estrategia, mecanismos y avances* (with L J. Garay), Bogotá, 1979; *Producción de café en Colombia* (with R. Junguito), Bogotá; 1991, *El comercio exterior y la política internacional del café* (with R. Junguito), Bogotá, 1993; *Instituciones e instrumentos de la política cafetera en Colombia* (with R. Junguito), Bogotá, 1997; *La globalización: Desafíos y oportunidades*; Bogotá, 2002; *Diálogos con economistas eminentes*, Jorge Pinto Books, New York, 2008.

Conversations with Great Economists

Diego Pizano

Conversations with Great Economists

*Friedrich A. Hayek, John Hicks, Nicholas Kaldor,
Leonid V. Kantorovich, Joan Robinson,
Paul A. Samuelson, Jan Tinbergen*

Jorge Pinto Books Inc.
New York

Conversations with Great Economists: Friedrich A. Hayek, John Hicks, Nicholas Kaldor, Leonid V. Kantorovich, Joan Robinson, Paul A. Samuelson, Jan Tinbergen

© Diego Pizano

Copyright of the edition © 2009 by Jorge Pinto Books Inc.

Originally published in Spanish with the title *Dialogos Con Economistas Eminentes*, First Spanish edition 1980 by Fondo de Cultura Económica, México D.F. Last Spanish edition in the US, 2008 by Jorge Pinto Books Inc.

All rights reserved. This book may not be reproduced in whole or in part, in any form (beyond copying permitted by Sections 107 and 108 of the United States Copyright Law, and except limited excerpts by reviewer for the public press), without written permission from Jorge Pinto Books Inc. 151 East 58th Street, New York, NY 10022.

Published by Jorge Pinto Books Inc., website: www.pintobooks.com

Cover design by Susan Hildebrand

Edition: Andrea Montejo.

Book design by Charles King, website: www.ckmm.com

ISBN: 1-934978-20-5
978-1-934978-20-7

This book is dedicated to Francisco Pizano de Brigard and Nicolás Gómez Dávila (1912–1994), in grateful acknowledgment for their important intellectual stimulation

Contents

About the Author i

Preface to the Second Edition. xi

Preface to the First Edition. xiii

A Conversation with Professor Friedrich A. Hayek 1

A Conversation with Professor John Hicks 25

A Conversation with Professor Nicholas Kaldor. 43

A Conversation with Professor Leonid V. Kantorovich 67

A Conversation with Professor Joan Robinson 81

A Conversation with Professor Paul A. Samuelson. 109

A Conversation with Professor Jan Tinbergen 129

Preface to the Second Edition

Many people, over the course of the last twenty-five years, have asked me how the idea of this project was born, and, especially, how in the world I was able to get such brilliant scholars to participate. I am going to try and give a brief answer to that query.

Between 1972 and 1974 I was carrying out postgraduate work at the University of Cambridge. At the time, the discipline of economics was passing through a particularly difficult time. Professor Joan Robinson spoke of the "second crisis in economic theory."[1] Professor John Hicks was busy writing about the crisis in Keynesian economics.[2] The world was facing the phenomena of stagflation, defined as the simultaneous presence of stagnation and inflation. At the same time, for a few years already, the most respected economists of Cambridge, England had been involved in a tough debate with the economists of MIT in Cambridge. (This, of course, was another Cambridge, in Massachusetts, USA.) Given this intellectual climate, it occurred to me that to set up dialogues with some of the most influential economists alive might be a good idea: they could speak about the actual state of things and they could offer their perspectives on our chosen discipline.

At the University of Cambridge I had the opportunity of discussing economic thought with the two tutors that were assigned to me, Professors John Eatwell—today a member of the House of Lords, and Master of Queens College in Cambridge—and Donald Moggridge the editor of the complete work of Keynes. On a few occasions I was able to converse with Professor Piero Sraffa and I once attended a seminar on the theory of growth given by Professor Nicholas Kaldor. I also had the opportunity of talking with Professor Joan Robinson and attended several of her lectures. In addition to this, I was able to go to conferences given by other renowned economists, such as Professors Kenneth Arrow and James Meade. With Michael Kucynski, instructor in economics and Fellow at Pembroke College, I had stimulating discussions. This postgraduate experience was fundamental in my project to prepare this book.

In Bogotá I had the privilege of discussing a wide variety of topics with several intellectual mentors: Nicolás Gómez-Dávila,

---
1. Joan Robinson, "The Second Crisis in Economic Theory," *A.E.R.*,1972.
2. John Hicks, *The Crisis in Keynesian Economics*, Oxford, 1974.

one of Latin America's great thinkers (in Germany, and in Italy, several professors consider him to be as important as Borges and Ortega y Gasset); Francisco Pizano, my father, and co-founder of the Universidad de los Andes, who worked with Le Corbusier on a development plan for Bogotá; and Professor Mario Laserna, co-founder of the Universidad de los Andes, and who had the privilege of discussing philosophy and physics with Professors Albert Einstein and John Von Neumann. The guidance and intellectual stimulation provided by these three remarkable men was of enormous importance to me.

In February 1976, I initiated the project by writing a letter to Professor Paul Samuelson at MIT, explaining my idea and indicating the types of topics I was interested in discussing with him. Much to my surprise, this distinguished professor—undoubtedly one of the most influential economists of the 20th century—showed interest in my idea and accepted my proposal. He replied, granting me an interview at his office at MIT in April 1976. This initial support was of course decisive for the future of the project. When I contacted the other professors to explain my idea, I was able to mention that Professor Samuelson had agreed to participate as well. Naturally, this was an important persuasive factor. To reinforce the presentation of the initiative I sent each Professor a brief essay examining their principle contributions to economics and formulating some questions and observations. This was to demonstrate that I had studied their work and to indicate that what I had in mind was in no way a superficial and casual conversation, but a structured dialogue.

I must say that this has been one of the most fulfilling and interesting projects I have carried out over the course of my life. To be in contact with these privileged minds, allowed me to learn a great deal about how some of the most creative economists of the 20th century thought. In addition, these conversations shed light on diverse aspects relating to the evolution of economics. I hope new readers will find this book equally stimulating.

Finally, I would like to acknowledge my gratitude to Jorge Pinto and Andrea Montejo for their pleasant and professional approach to preparing this second edition and to Denise Michelsen and Darrell Hueth, who took the trouble of carefully reviewing the whole text and suggesting improvements.

DIEGO PIZANO
Bogotá, August 2009

Preface to the First Edition

The present volume gathers together a series of dialogues sustained with a group of internationally renowned economists, conversations held with the intention of clarifying contemporary economic theory, its present state and development. With this objective in mind, not only were general aspects of economics discussed, but also some of the specific contributions of each of the scholars who agreed to participate. It must be made clear that in the context of a small-scale work such as this, it was only possible to make reference to a limited set of ideas. Even so, and given the unsuspected complexity of the topic, the dialogue—a form of expression no longer much cultivated in the 20th century—was deemed to be the best exploratory vehicle.

Dialogue endows even the most obtuse and arid material with a degree of life and clarity that would not easily been reached if the chosen mode of expression had been a long written treatise on the evolution of economic thought. Dialogue is an exercise that forces participants to keep to the essential. Matters that at first glance might have seemed incomprehensible become comprehensible. This explains the methodology employed. But, what can be said of the book's scope and contents?

The original impulse behind this project was the realization that there is a growing distance between the theoretical developments in economics and their practical applicability. As Professor Samuelson says somewhere, economists are trained as if they were athletes preparing themselves for a race that is never going to take place. This situation is obvious to anyone who has studied economics at a theoretical level and has been in the position of having to formulate recommendations in political economy.

Yet, this gap between theory and practice is even more evident for those in the position of observing the English phenomenon first-hand. England has produced a high percentage of the world's most celebrated economists. Nonetheless, the country operates at this time (1974–1980) under an economic system that very few people in this world would describe as ideal. This is as paradoxical as if a community with the world's best doctors were to have, at the same time, the world's sickest population.

This situation as described has, inevitably, led the practitioners of the discipline to meditate on the evolution, method, problems and perspectives of their chosen field. And, as the creators and philosophers of mathematics have taught us, in order to see a discipline clearly, it is necessary to observe it from afar. This, in turn, explains the presence of some references to epistemology and other topics that do not, strictly speaking, pertain to the rigorously technical realm of economics.

Some of my colleagues have asked me, in a slightly skeptical tone, why, in some of these conversations, I refer to certain areas of knowledge that are so far removed from the discipline of economics itself. In reality the answer has a lot to do with that fundamental difference that separates economics from physics. In order to become a respected physicist, it is indispensable for one to focus on a well-defined field and deeply examine a very specific aspect of a determined problem. In order to become an economist it is also necessary for one to be capable of adequately formulating a specific problem. In addition, however, it is important to place that problem in its temporal, spatial, psychological, philosophical, logical, legal and ethical dimension. Obviously, this is clearly a consequence of the fact that human behavior is much more complex than the behavior of inert matter. It may well be that, if the strictly technical economists were to add these dimensions to their problem analysis, they would stop being athletes in training for a race that they are never going to run.

Before we plunge into the dialogues I have had the honor to be a part of, I would like to express my gratitude to some of the people who, in one way or another, contributed to the realization of this work. First of all I must highlight the incredible intellectual generosity of the scholars who, in accepting my invitation, interrupted their multiple activities, setting aside some time to consider some of the issues presented (in some cases via a previously submitted written piece of work).

I would also like to mention Nicolás Gómez-Dávila, from Bogotá, who helped me understand some very complicated issues in the field of epistemology. Professor Albert O. Hirschman, from the Institute of Advanced Studies at Princeton, read all of the dialogues and stimulated me with his comments. Finally my thanks also to Carlos Caballero, Roberto Junguito and Jorge Ospina, my old research partners at Fedesarrollo in Bogotá, who showed great enthusiasm for this project from the very beginning.

DIEGO PIZANO
Bogotá, January, 1980

A Conversation with Professor Friedrich A. Hayek

In 1977 I spent some time at the University of Oxford writing an essay on the economic history of Colombia. At the time I had the opportunity of meeting Professor Sir John Hicks, one of the most important British economists, and Professor Sir Karl Popper (who was not connected with Oxford but lived nearby at Buckinghamshire), one of the most outstanding philosophers of the 20th century. When I explained my project on contemporary economic theory to them, they suggested I contact Professor Hayek. I had read some of his books and had been intrigued by the manner in which he integrated elements derived from law, philosophy and psychology into his economic theories. Early in 1979 I was invited to work as a researcher at the Institut für Iberoamerika Kunde in Hamburg, Germany. It was from Hamburg that I wrote to this distinguished scholar requesting that he grant me an interview and become part of my survey. A few days later he responded, inviting me to come to his home in Freiburg, Germany, so we could talk. I visited him in July 1979. As I entered his private library the Professor greeted me warmly and sat me down in a huge armchair. Behind him I could see two oil paintings, portraits of his favorite thinkers: David Hume and Adam Smith.

Friedrich A. Hayek (1899–1992) studied at the University of Vienna, where he earned a Doctorate in both Law and Political Science. His father had been a Biology Professor and one of his cousins was the famous philosopher, Ludwig Wittgenstein. After working a few years with the government, he was named Director of the Austrian Institute for Economic Research. In 1931 he was named Professor at the University of London, and in 1950 he went to the University of Chicago where he was Professor of Social and Moral Sciences. Several years later he was appointed Professor Emeritus at the University of Freiburg in West Germany. This is what he was up to when I met him. Doctor Hayek was a member of the British Academy and he received the Nobel Prize in Economics in 1974. He published several books in the fields of economics, philosophy, psychology and law. (See *Bibliography*.) His influence in the last quarter of the XXth century was notable. Many analysts have pointed out that he was influential in the fall of the Berlin wall, the collapse of the Soviet Union, and the political economics developed by Reagan and Thatcher, as well as in several Eastern European countries.

His publications include: *The Pure Theory of Capital, The Sensory Order, Studies in Philosophy, Politics and Economics; The Road to Serfdom; Law, Legislation and Liberty* (three volumes).

The Conversation

Diego Pizano: Economics, to a certain extent, with the establishment of a Nobel Memorial Prize, has attained the status previously awarded only to the natural sciences. Nevertheless, many professional economists at the highest theoretical levels have shown deep dissatisfaction with the progress and the state of knowledge of economic theory. You, yourself, have stated in your Nobel Prize lecture that economists have little cause for pride and that they have made a mess of things. I would like to examine this situation; is there a deep crisis in economic theory and economic policy? Or is there just a temporary lack of confidence in the strength of the discipline?

May I take the liberty of providing a preliminary answer to this very large question by pointing out some unresolved problems theoreticians have been unable to solve and which are the main cause of the situation described? I shall be very brief in my presentation since most of the problems I shall mention are well known. I consider that theorists have failed in explaining and understanding some of the following problems, which seem to be rather important in the real world:

(a) **Stagflation:** According to Professor Samuelson[3] there is no satisfactory theory to explain the simultaneous existence of inflation and recession; this is one of the greatest challenges theorists are now facing. Phillips curves are certainly not considered seriously in most countries.

(b) **Economies of scale:** According to the OECD and other studies, decreasing costs dominate the picture in the industrial sector of the world economy (particularly in steel, petrochemi-

---
3. See Diego Pizano, "A Conversation with Professor Paul A. Samuelson," in this book.

cals, automobile, electricity generation, etc.) Yet no theorist has been able to incorporate them in general equilibrium systems because they have rather destructive consequences.

(c) **Distribution of Income:** According to Joan Robinson, there is no theory which satisfactorily explains the determinants of the distribution of income ("The Second Crisis of Economic Theory," AER). As we all know, this was the goal for economics as a discipline following Ricardo.

(d) **Uncertainty:** The assumption of perfect foresight made by many theorists is regarded as extremely unrealistic and yet it is very difficult to let go. Some claim that Keynes, with his liquidity preference function, managed to do so but this is still debated.

(e) **Determinants of economic growth:** Scholars such as Professor Kuznets of Harvard University have made important advances in the field of economic history. Nonetheless, explanations of the so-called residual fall short and it is still too large, up to 50 percent in some exercises!

(f) **Endogenization of the technical progress function:** There has been, a lot of work on this area ranging from Schumpeter's business cycle theories to Labini's oligopoly models. However, there is still a great deal to be learnt about the interaction between technical progress and economic development. A particularly difficult problem is to postulate a realistic technical progress function. Perhaps this cannot be done at all since the process of scientific discovery is not deterministic as Popper has so clearly shown (*The Poverty of Historicism*, London, 1957).

(g) **Theory of decision-making and collective choice:** In this area Arrow's impossibility theorem has created rather difficult problems and no obvious solution seems to be at hand.

(h) **Oligopoly:** Most theorists agree in that there is no single theory of oligopoly that explains the formation of prices in important sectors of the world economy such as the international motorcar industry. Or to cite a more striking example, the game multinational oil companies, governments and oil producers are involved in.

(i) **Crisis of Keynesian economics:** This, as we all know, is the title of a recent book written by Sir John Hicks. And of course you have been critical of Keynesian theories since their appearance in the thirties.

It is evident that every serious discipline faces a long list of unresolved problems that constitute the main reason for its very existence. The issue is, to what extent is the discipline of economics passing through one of those critical phases that, according to Kuhn might provide the stimulus for a change of paradigm (*The Structure of Scientific Revolutions*).

What is your reaction to this introductory presentation?

Professor Hayek: All the problems you have mentioned are connected. So I prefer to treat them all from a general perspective instead of discussing one by one. Let me begin by answering your question concerning the existence of a crisis in economic theory. I think the answer is that economics is now recovering from a long period of decline that was caused by the transition it attempted to make from microeconomics to macroeconomics. Keynes is clearly responsible for this change although he was by no means alone. But he has contributed, perhaps unintentionally, more than anybody else to the spread of aggregative theorizing, which is the essence of macroeconomics. I personally believe that only microeconomics really explains anything, but it is of necessity limited in its power of explanation. And, precisely because of these limitations in its explanatory capacity, economists decided to construct a new system which they thought to be more scientific: macroeconomics. This attempt, however, was based on erroneous hypothesis and has been a complete failure. I must confess that for the past thirty years I have not been interested in most of the subjects which have occupied the minds of the majority of economists: macroeconomics, welfare economics, employment theory, input-output analysis, the theory of growth, etc. I have not taken part in any of these discussions, nor have I made any contribution to them. That is why my prestige as a theorist has declined over the last decades. Many economists are now beginning to realize that their approach was mistaken and they are coming back to me.

Let me turn now to what I regard as the main problem of economic theory, which will also explain that what we can achieve must absolutely be limited. The basic task of economic theory is to really explain how we bring about an adaptation to the unknown. There is no question that the constant changes of economic activity are caused by a large number of factors that nobody knows as a whole. We are therefore constantly acting in order to adapt ourselves to factors that are unknown to us and for this purpose we can only use limited and fragmented information. To put it in a more concrete form: we work in order to serve the needs of millions of people of whom we know nothing, and for this purpose we use the activities of other millions of people who supply raw materials and instruments that we need for our production. Again, we know nothing about them. This has become possible by the spontaneous evolution of a system of communications which, by means of signals, tells economic agents what to do in order to adapt to events we know very little about. The system is the market and the signals are the prices.

My whole concept of economics is based on the idea that we have to explain how prices operate as signals, telling people what they ought to do in particular circumstances. The approach to this problem has been blocked by a cost or labor theory of value, which assumes that prices are determined by the technical conditions of production only. The important question is to explain how the interaction of a great number of people, each possessing only limited knowledge, will bring about an order that could only be achieved by deliberate direction taken by somebody who has the combined knowledge of all these individuals. However, central planning cannot take direct account of particular circumstances of time and place. Additionally, every individual has important bits of information which cannot possibly be conveyed to a central authority in statistical form. In a system in which the knowledge of relevant data is dispersed among millions of agents, prices can act to coordinate the separate actions of different individuals.

Given this context, it is intellectually not satisfactory to attempt to establish causal relations between aggregates or averages in the manner in which the discipline of macroeconomics has attempted to do. Individuals do not make decisions on the basis of partial knowledge of magnitudes such as the total amount of production, or the total quantity of money. Aggregative theorizing leads nowhere.

At the same time there is a strong tendency among social scientists towards scientism, that is to say, to adopt a methodology which has the appearance of being scientific and which is based on the assumption that it is desirable to replace spontaneous processes by deliberate human control. This erroneous view has lead to a drastic decline in the importance and relevance of economic theory and explains the crisis you have pointed out.

D.P.: I think it is not clear that Keynes was treating economics as a natural science. Not only did he attack Tinbergen's econometric work, but in a letter written to Harrod (*Collected Works, vol. XIV*) he strongly emphasizes that economics is a moral discipline concerned with introspection, expectations and psychological uncertainties. It is also interesting to note that, despite having been trained as a mathematician, he rejected the possibility of constructing mathematical models on the grounds they would distort reality.

Professor Hayek: That is certainly paradoxical. I agree. Keynes was aware of the differences that exist between the social and natural sciences. He was a man of great intellect but of a rather limited knowledge of economic theory. When I had the opportunity of discussing economics with him, I was taken aback when many surprising gaps in his knowledge appeared. He had not read Ricardo's work carefully, for instance.

The theory guiding monetary and financial policy in many countries over the last thirty years is based on Keynesian ideas, and it is based on the assertion that there is a simple positive correlation between total employment and the size of aggregate demand for goods and services. This has lead to the false belief that we can permanently assure full employment by maintaining the total money expenditure at an appropriate level. This Keynesian doctrine has caused great harm and is responsible, to a great extent, for the problems the international economy has experienced in the seventies.

D.P.: It is difficult to believe, however, that if nothing had been done after the Crash of 1929 in the United States, that full employment would have been restored automatically by laissez-faire policies. After all, Keynesian policies did reduce unemployment drastically in England and other countries after the Great Depression.

Professor Hayek: No economist who lived through Great Depression, as I, myself did, could ever underestimate the gravity of the problem of unemployment. I have not denied that in some extreme cases and, mainly because of political considerations, employment can be increased by monetary expansion. But it can only be increased for a short period of time and one must be aware that by doing this, things will get much worse in the long run. Present unemployment is the direct and inevitable consequence of the so-called full-employment policies of the last twenty years. The fundamental cause of unemployment is the deviation of prices and wages from what they would be if we had a free market and a stable currency. However, I must admit, when asked to provide the empirical structure of prices and wages which would ensure full employment and stable prices, I have to declare that I do not have that information.

As I stated in my Nobel Prize lecture, most contemporary economists overlook the inherent limitations of our numerical knowledge. It is interesting to note, however, that in the XVIth century, people like Luis Molina anticipated in a remarkable way, one of the most important principles we must always take into account:[4] particular prices depend on so many circumstances that their value can never be known to man but only to God.

Economists have to plead ignorance to the sort of facts on which physicists are expected to give information. This is due to the fact that we have to deal with complex structures and with a much greater number of interacting variables than physicists.

D.P.: I consider that social reality is more complicated than natural phenomena, not only because one has to deal with a much greater number of variables, but also because of their greater variability, lesser uniformity and the greater difficulty that lies in isolating one factor at a time. I pointed this out to Professor Popper in a recent conversation and he replied:[5] "There is no doubt that the analysis of any specific social situation is made very difficult by its complexity. But the same holds true for physical situations and biological ones. The difficulties associated with the understanding of the functioning of the human brain are astonishing. I could say that I have never encountered a problem so complicated."

I challenged his assertion by saying that the human world involves the natural world and not the other way around. This means that if one wanted to have a full model of the behavior of an oligopolist one would need to have a reasonable understanding of how the brain works. He said that the task of integrating the knowledge we have about the brain and what is known of the behavior of an oligopolist appeared to be very difficult and that he did not know of any economist trying to do this.

---

4. Luis Molina, *De iustitia et iure*, Colonia, 1595.
5. See Diego Pizano, "A Conversation with Professor Karl Popper," unpublished manuscript, Bogotá, 1977.

Professor Hayek: I have derived my epistemological position and many of my philosophical ideas from Karl Popper who has been my friend for many years. But let me say that insofar the degree of complexity of social phenomena is concerned, he has not yet grasped the point I have made. I think that the distinction introduced by Dr. W. Weaver (formerly working at the Rockefeller Foundation) has not been, sufficiently appreciated. He proposed distinguishing between phenomena of unorganized complexity, such as the ones we find in physics, and those of organized complexity, such as the ones we find in social sciences such as economics. In physics—and the clearest instance is thermodynamics—one has to deal with enormous complexity and it is unorganized. We have many individual elements interacting (molecules) but instead of obtaining specific information about the individual elements, one can use probabilities. In other words, one can substitute statistics for specific information on the behavior of each molecule. But when it comes to organized phenomena with high degrees of complexity, one cannot substitute statistics for information about individual events because the whole thing depends on how individual elements are related to each other. Therefore we do not have the recourse that physics still has of inserting probabilities of occurrence when faced with a lack of information. And this is where one is reduced to systems theory, cybernetics or communications theory as it is called in the social sciences. In this context one has to show how complex structures are built by the relationships that exist between their elements. In this sense, in biology and the social sciences complexity sets limits to what we can explain. The human brain can never explain itself because to explain something of such a degree of complexity, one would need to have a structure of a higher degree of complexity. And of course we do not have a super-brain to explain our own brain.

D.P.: Professor Popper also pointed out that one must take into account that in most social situations there is an important element of rationality, and this simplifies, according to him, the subject matter of social sciences considerably because it makes possible the construction of simple models of actions and interactions.

Professor Hayek: I would say that the assumption of rationality implies that others' minds are similar to our own. This is why we can understand it to a certain extent. But this is not understanding in detail. We never know the kind of processes that take place in the minds of people in particular moments; therefore, all we can come to grasp is the pattern of a process or some of its general characteristics but not its specific manifestations at a particular moment. In fact we can, perhaps, suggest what kinds of things a particular oligopolist is likely to do in a specific situation but we cannot predict what he will do.

Rational behavior is not a premise of economic theory, although it is usually presented as such. The essential point to be made is that competition will make it necessary for people to act rationally if they are willing to maintain their position or if they wish to improve it.

D.P.: Coming back to the analysis of the market, I would like to ask a rather obvious question. If economies of scale are as important as many studies indicate, and if uncertainty is a rule and not the exception, then wouldn't the free operation of market forces lead us, not to the best allocation of resources as Pareto postulated, but to various monopolistic organizations as well as various distortions derived from market failures?

Professor Hayek: I think the basic misconception is to speak of the so-called "best" allocation of resources. What is the best? In common economics it is defined as what would be if we knew everything. Economists operate with the fictitious assumption that all the relevant data is known, but this is totally unrealistic. Nobody knows all the data. What we have is widely dispersed knowledge, which cannot be concentrated in one mind. To call the situation—which would use all the knowledge available—"optimal" is nonsense because it is by definition a non-achievable solution. Our problem is not the full utilization of all knowledge but the best use we can achieve with any known institutional structure. In that sense, some oligopolistic (and even monopolistic situations), represent the best possible utilization of knowledge that we can achieve. Even the action of a monopolist can be extremely beneficial. Consider the following example, which has just occurred to me. Somebody discovers a very cheap source of a raw material, say some strategic mineral product, and he is the sole owner of it. And he is able to produce it cheaper than anybody else. He then comes into the market, not selling it at marginal costs, but for just a little less than all the other suppliers and so he completely captures the market. Theoretically, it would be possible for him to bring it down to, let us say, one tenth of the original price but even if he doesn't do that, and even if he is making an extraordinary profit, he is still enormously benefiting society because, obviously, he is producing the total output at a lower cost than before. In some situations this is the best we can achieve.

D.P.: But one must remember that the critics of the market say that the best argument against the utilization of market forces is the Great Depression. How can one argue that the economic situation of the Crash of 1929 represents a reasonable state of affairs or is the best we can achieve?

Professor Hayek: My whole work started, as you know, with the analysis of business cycles. One has to determine to what extent depressions are the result of the operation of market forces, or if they are the result of a falsification of the market process mainly by monetary policy. I do not believe that we would have major industrial fluctuations if it were not for our present banking system, which in turn depends on the government monopoly of the supply of money. If we had allowed the market to develop the amount of money at which it works efficiently we would no longer have any major fluctuations or depressions. I have been driven into proposing the denationalization of money, which is a perfectly consistent development of my ideas. I am convinced that the present monetary system—which has been created by government intervention—prevented the development of another kind of system. I am also convinced, on other grounds, that it would be politically impossible for a government to pursue a good monetary policy because it would deprive it of the power of helping particular groups. I am convinced an efficient monetary system is feasible once we abolish the government monopoly of the issuing of money. This would lead to competition and eliminate extreme fluctuations in economic cycles in the long run. Anyhow, depressions are not the result of the operation of the market. They are the result of government controls, particularly in the sphere of monetary policy.

D.P.: Your proposal to denationalize money is interesting. But don't you think people might lose confidence in the banking system if they realize there is no central authority backing up the monetary currency?

Professor Hayek: I think people will realize that it is in the best interest of the banks to provide stable money as the survival of their profitable business depends on it in order for the system to work. Any bank that fails to do so will be driven out of business by its competitors.

In my opinion, instead of promoting a European monetary union, we should eliminate all restrictions on the circulation of money and allow the establishment of foreign banks in all countries. National currencies would be allowed to compete freely in all countries. Who would use British Sterling in England if he could use Swiss Francs?

D.P.: A significant group of people is hostile to the idea of leaving market forces flow freely because they think it is not possible to reconcile productive efficiency and distributive justice without the intervention of the state. What is your reaction to this point of view?

Professor Hayek: For the past fifteen years I have been trying to understand what social justice is and I must say I have failed to do so. This phrase has no meaning whatsoever when applied to a society of free men. There can be no distributive justice where no one distributes. I have devoted a whole volume to this question (*The Mirage of Social Justice, London,* 1976) since it has become a standard for guiding political action and I consider that the term "social justice" does not have an intelligible definition. This, of course, is hard for many people to believe. The main point that needs to be stressed is that social justice only makes conceptual sense in a centrally planned economy but is inapplicable to the results of a spontaneous process. Once the vacuity of the term is recognized, it is dishonest to continue to use it.

On the other hand, there can be no doubt that most of those who have built fortunes in the form of new enterprises and industrial plants have thereby benefited more people through the expansion of productive employment than if they had given their initial resources directly to the poor. What socialists want to gain is the power to allocate resources in an arbitrary way, and by doing so, destroy personal freedom. The great merit of the market is that it deprives everyone of such power.

D.P.: Another frequent attack against market forces comes from people who think that these may work in the context of advanced industrial societies but won't stimulate economic development in poorer countries.

Professor Hayek: In highly developed economic systems competition is very important as a process of exploration in which agents search for unexploited opportunities and, once these are discovered, can be used by others. I am convinced this is true to an even greater extent in less developed countries. The chief problem of such countries is to discover what material and human resources are available. For that purpose, competition is the best procedure we know. Many developing countries lament their apparent lack of entrepreneurial spirit. Yet, it is very clear that the cause of this situation is not an unchangeable characteristic of the inhabitants but the direct consequence of restraining market forces.

D.P.: I agree; economists in developing countries need to think much more about the creative forces generated by a free market and not just focus on the function of allocating resources. But let me now return to a brief discussion of business cycles by briefly comparing the Crash of 1929 and the so-called Nixon–Ford cycle (1974–75).

There is now a growing awareness among the members of the economic profession that business cycles deserve to be explained and that they are not just historical curiosities. The economic contraction that started in 1929 has been the worst in history. Yet very few economists have tried to understand this event by applying the various business cycle theories. It may well be because the possibility of testing alternative theories is limited given the small number of truly independent observations. However, I consider that history is the only approximation economists have to a laboratory to test the validity of alternative theories. It is surprising to discover that the crisis of 1929 is still not fully understood. Naturally there are interpretations: Friedman and Schwartz argue, for instance, in *A Monetary History of the United States,* that the absence of a concerted expansionary macroeconomic policy was to an important extent one of the principle causes behind the magnitude of the contraction. To what extent do you agree?

On the other hand, what light does the study of the 1929 contraction shed on the 1974–5 cycle? In answering it might be useful to take into account some similarities and discrepancies which result from a comparative analysis of both periods. At the risk of oversimplifying, one could argue that some of the major similarities are:

(i) Real money stock behaves in an expansionary manner in both periods.
(ii) In both periods GNP, real consumption, residential construction and stock exchange indexes dropped significantly.
(iii) Sharp changes in the terms of trade, instability of foreign exchange markets and large shifts in international lending were characteristic of both periods.

However, there are very large discrepancies such as the following:

(i) The price history is very different (deflation vs. inflation).
(ii) Gold standard vs. floating exchange rates.
(iii) OPEC, obviously, is a new factor.
(iv) The role of developing countries is different.

Given these differences, to what extent could a single framework be useful in trying to explain the two cycles?

Professor Hayek: Let me just make some comments to this rather complex question. In the two years before the American Crash of 1929, the Federal Reserve System had used credit expansion to prolong the boom, which had threatened to cease in 1927. To a large extent this was done to support the British pound, which was in difficulties. It was assumed that if the dollar was not too strong, the British situation would be easier. At the time, I was so convinced that this was an overexpansion that, as you perhaps know, at the beginning of 1929 I predicted the American Crash. One could foresee this very clearly. But then, of course, it is important to point out a second aspect. There is no doubt, and in this I agree with Milton Friedman, that once the Crash had occurred, the Federal Reserve System pursued a silly deflationary policy. I am not only against inflation but I am also against deflation! So, once again, a badly programmed monetary policy prolonged the depression. One consequence of this policy was, of course, the fact that confidence was destroyed. In 1930, when the first signs of revival were beginning to appear, President Roosevelt took America off the gold standard. This event caused such a disturbance in the monetary market that it greatly accelerated the crisis.

Let me go into the question you raised regarding flexible exchange rates. The origin of the demand for flexible exchange rates came entirely from people who wanted more expansion and opposed the limits which were determined by the existence of fixed exchange rates. That is why, at that time, I strongly objected to flexible exchange rates because they were being promoted merely to make an inflationary policy possible. Later I, myself, was forced to admit that flexible exchange rates are necessary for the opposite purpose, that is to say, for protection against imported inflation. Here, in Germany, people argued that it was a mistake to maintain fixed exchange rates. If one wants to restrain other countries from inflating too much, one should introduce the system of flexible exchanges. This issue raises the question: do we want national or international money? And there I am in favor of international money. In the thirties, I was convinced that the only instrument available for providing monetary stability was the gold standard. I now think it is no longer practicable, not only have national governments shown an unwillingness to play according to the rules of the gold standard but, even more important, because a return to the standard would lead to a high degree of fluctuations in the value of gold and it would become an unsuitable monetary standard.

D.P.: What do you consider to be the main lesson one can extract from an analysis of the Great Depression?

Professor Hayek: I think that the artificial expansion of the boom led to the depression. Then authorities made things worse by a process of deliberate contraction. It is very clear to me that the monetary authorities caused the 1929 Crash and they are also responsible for subsequent cycles. I do not agree with Friedman on the causes but I do agree with his criticism of the Federal Reserve policy that followed. They made a great mistake before and after the crisis.

D.P.: Some people have argued that one of the main causes of the Great Depression was the great drop that was observed in the activity level in the construction industry. Do you think this played an important role?

Professor Hayek: I should say the construction industry had been over-stimulated before and so it reached a level at which it could not be maintained. Afterward, the breakdown became inevitable.

D.P.: And what could you say of the role played by the drastic drop in the stock exchange indexes? Could it be considered an important cause or was it more an effect?

Professor Hayek: I think that in my scheme the stock exchange adjusted to the expectations of continued growth of investment and when the Federal Reserve System was no longer willing to finance projects, investment decreased drastically and so the stock exchange collapsed. The stock exchange had to react to the disappointment of unfulfilled expectations regarding the possibilities of investment.

D.P.: Coming back to the analysis of the importance of market forces as tools for discovery and as stimulators of economic growth, I would like to tell you that Professor Ludwig Erhard asserted, in a conference given at Universidad de los Andes in Bogotá in 1969, that the German economic miracle was not a miracle, but the result of hard work of millions of people who managed to coordinate their actions. Do you think German prosperity has been the result of a society working in agreement with the essential principles you have put forward in your trilogy, *Law, Legislation and Liberty*?

Professor Hayek: Germany is a very imperfect example, but it is certainly better than any other. Let me say, that I entirely agree with Erhard's assertion since the way the economy behaved was exactly what he had expected when he scrapped all price controls in 1948. This was a decisive moment. It is clear to me that there was nothing unexpected about the consequences. The original German recovery was entirely due to the return to a much more liberal economic system. But then there were other favorable circumstances and one of the most important circumstances, which is not generally understood, was the good sense of the German trade unions, which once again, can be historically explained. Trade union leaders remembered two great inflations. So, when union leaders asked for salary increases over and above productivity, the only thing employers had to point out was that higher wages would create the conditions for accelerated inflation. The trade unions acted in a very responsible way and, in keeping with their own interest in the long run, the unions accepted their responsibility in helping control inflation.

This sensible generation of trade unionists was in charge until fairly recently. This is an advantage Germany is now losing because the older generation, the generation that remembers hyperinflation, is being replaced by a new one. This is bad news for the country. Fortunately, the German constitution excludes granting trade unions the excessive powers they have in England. Here, there is practically no possibility of violent picketing or any use of force. This still helps the country and Germany has, on the whole, the most liberal constitution in the world—even though it is still far from being ideal, in my opinion. It is possible that similar conditions may be found in Belgium, but I find it hard to mention another country where the conditions are as favorable as in Germany. Of course, one can point out various places where economic miracles have occurred because of economic freedom, places such as Hong Kong and Singapore and, to a certain extent, even in South Korea, which is by no means a liberal economy. Not that they restrict the actions of entrepreneurs but the problem is that the government subsidizes too much. But, on the whole, the South Korean miracle (which is comparable to the Japanese miracle) is due to the free market functioning of the entire system.

D.P.: One can observe a very clear growth of public involvement in the economic life of most countries around the world. A key question for many developing countries is the extent to which the state should protect the private sector (through easy loans, tax rebates, tariffs, export incentives, etc.), particularly when there is uncertainty and certain risks need to be taken into account when making investment decisions. As you know, Arrow and Lind (*Issues in Public Finance*) prefer to recommend public investment rather than grant subsidies to the private sector. They think that providing direct subsidies does not alter the costs of risk bearing and therefore it encourages investments which are inefficient when the costs of risks are taken into consideration. It is easy to see that Arrow and Lind assume that the government can ignore the costs of risk bearing and, if the project has a high social rate of return, they would recommend public planners to undertake the investment even if the project ultimately proves to be inefficient.

It is clear to me that an excessive level of subsidies may create undesirable distortions and may lead to an abuse of public funds. However, an increase of public investment can create even greater difficulties, namely inefficiency and corruption. So perhaps production subsidies are justified in certain cases.

Professor Hayek: Maybe subsidies are justified in order to prevent the harm the government does in other ways! I consider that governments should stay out of risky projects. If a sensible taxation policy exists, one that does not excessively burden the private sector, it will generate a reasonable amount of funds for the government. On the other hand, if in the past, the governments of several countries had not discouraged investment so much, today no encouragement would be needed. If there is an adequate balance between risk and profits, the private sector will invest and there is no need for public investment.

D.P.: What would the role of the state be in your ideal economic system?

Professor Hayek: First of all, to provide a general legal framework that is most conducive to the functioning of the market. This means the gradual improvement of the rules of private and commercial law. Then there is the task of providing, outside the market, certain goods and services for some people who are not able to earn a minimum level of income in the market. But that should not be done by interfering with the market; it should be done outside the market. People who cannot generate a basic income for covering their fundamental needs should get a uniform compensation from the state.

On the other hand, as I have attempted to make clear in my book, *The Political Order of a Free People* (London, 1979), I am not advocating a mini-state confined to the enforcement of the law and to defend citizens from external enemies.

The government ought to use its power for raising funds by taxation to provide collective goods which cannot be adequately supplied by the market (parks, maps, certification of the quality of products, etc.) and to control negative external effects such as pollution.

D.P.: Your idea about the minimum level of income is interesting. To what extent is it equivalent to Friedman's negative income tax?

Professor Hayek: I believe, on the whole, that Friedman's proposal is a solution. I never specialized on the questions of public finance, but I think that Friedman's proposal can be made compatible with a flat tax rate. It need not be really progressive. Below a certain level of income you supplement people's income, and, above a certain point, you deduct on a constant basis. With this qualification, I would accept Friedman's proposal. My disagreement with him on monetary policy obscures the fact that on most other issues I very much agree with him. Things like his idea of establishing coupons for education and the negative income tax are brilliant.

D.P.: In Latin America Friedman's ideas are particularly associated with the economic policy of Chile.

Professor Hayek: Oh, yes, I visited Chile some time ago and I found that the country is being governed by members of Friedman's seminar!

D.P.: What was your impression of Chile? Are Friedman's theories working well when translated into practice?

Professor Hayek: The economic system is working marvelously and the recovery is extraordinary. I did not see the system of political control in enough detail to have a serious opinion about it, but I can say that the economy is much freer in comparison to what it had been for a very long time. I also think that the way in which Chile is covered by the international press is scandalous.

D.P.: Turning the discussion to a related topic, I want to tell you that I had the chance to discuss with Professor Tinbergen[6] his theory of the convergence of economic systems at a global level. It appears that the gradual rediscovery of the market by the socialist states—in the sense that they are complementing their planning activities with a certain degree of decentralization of their economic system and the simultaneous growth of the public sector in western economies—will lead to a sort of mixed economy in many states. Do you believe in this tendency towards the convergence of economic systems in the world today?

---

6. See Diego Pizano, "A Conversation with Profesor Jan Tinbergen," in this book.

Professor Hayek: I do not believe an actual tendency exists. It is true there has been a movement in socialist countries towards decentralization since a strictly planned economy could not be made to work, and it is also true that over the past thirty years the western economies have moved away from a free system. I do not think the latter will continue because, once the State is committed to the degree of interference we have experienced in the last years, and that has driven states to such stupid measures, there will be a reaction in the West towards greater freedom of action. I do not think you can expect the present generation of politicians to understand this with a few exceptions. The present English government has a leader who really understands this. Germany has the great fortune of having a socialist party with a chief who is not a socialist! Schmidt is clearly not a socialist. The general phrase which I always use in connection to this is: there is such a reaction among the younger generation against these interventionist tendencies that if politicians do not destroy civilization in the next twenty years there will be a return to a free economy in the Western world. This revival of what we in Europe call liberal ideas (in America liberal ideas imply advocating government interference) is extraordinary, even in countries like France which, for a long time, did not have liberal groups and where now a strong group of liberal economists is acting. It is true, as well, of Germany and it is very true for the United States. For the most part, these are people in their twenties and thirties but it has changed the situation in the world completely. I always like to say that when I was very young only the very old men believed in the market economy. When I was middle-aged nobody believed in the market economy, except me. And, now that I am very old, it is only the very young who believe in it! That makes me optimistic in the long run, but the immediate future is still rather dark. I feel that the government trend is still going towards more control. But, as I said, there is a reaction occurring among the younger generation and that is where I place my hope for the future.

D.P.: In your introductory remarks to your book *Philosophy, Politics and Economics* (1967) you said that you realized at an early stage of your career that if you wanted to get into the field of economic policy you had to equip yourself with a wide range of knowledge quite apart from technical economics and mathematics. So you found it necessary to become a philosopher of science, a political theorist, and had to do a great deal of research on legal, historical and psychological matters. Now that you have undertaken this very complete and lengthy preparation do you feel ready to offer advice on economic policy?

Professor Hayek: On the principles of economic policy, certainly. I am no longer sufficiently informed about the facts of any particular country to wish to have anything to do with particular measures. So I am operating entirely by expressing my ideas. My aim is to make politically possible what today is not yet politically possible.

D.P.: I am asking you this question because I think it is very important for the design of economic studies at our universities. To what extent could some of the failures of the economic policy of the last forty years be prevented in the future by giving decision makers a multi-dimensional training ranging from epistemology to the theory of justice, in addition to purely technical economic subjects?

Professor Hayek: I am convinced economists would do much less harm if they had this training. But you cannot expect the normal, practical economist to have time for this. However, it is an important topic to introduce in the main textbooks sections, which would give students the possibility of dealing with philosophical problems and with legal matters—matters that most members of this profession have never had the chance to handle. They are in the unfortunate position of not being able to spend half their lives on philosophical studies.

I have been very lucky in my career. I had twenty years at the London School of Economics and then I was asked to Chicago where I was a member of the so-called Committee on the Social Sciences, which dedicated itself to the issues that arise at the crossroads of different disciplines, and I could do whatever I pleased. I had time to educate myself philosophically. This is not the position of the normal economist. What can be done in terms of the discipline's curriculum is to provide students with general introductions to a wide range of issues. I am just starting a new book whose title will be *The Immense Conceit*, which deals entirely with the philosophical foundations on which our present policy is based. The analysis takes into account the conception of economics as being an adaptation to the unknown—that is the key phrase.

D.P.: I am looking forward to reading this book you announce. I would like to ask you what you consider to be your greatest contribution to economic theory. Machlup (*Essays on Hayek*) considers that your Theory of Capital is your greatest work since it contains "the most penetrating thoughts on the subject that have ever been published." Do you agree with his assessment?

Professor Hayek: I do not agree. The point at which I gained a new approach on which all my further development started was a lecture I gave in London in 1936, the same year the *General Theory* appeared, and which was titled "Economics and Knowledge." That piece of work contains the germs of all my further developments. I found that work in quite different fields such as the theory of capital, trade cycle theory and socialism all lead me to the same fundamental philosophical idea I expressed for the first time in that 1936 essay.

D.P.: You shared the Nobel Prize with Professor Myrdal and he reacted to your Nobel Memorial lecture stating that he had never thought seriously about epistemology. What was your reaction to Myrdal's lecture?

Professor Hayek: Well, it confirmed for me that it seems to be impossible to penetrate the minds of people who start their analysis with certain socialist prejudices. By this I mean certain philosophical prejudices, the idea that you can shape the world according to your will in every detail. I am aware that the world we live in is a result of a process of evolution that we cannot control. We may try to tinker with it (to use Popper's phrase), that is to say, we can try to improve it here and there, but the whole development is beyond our control. The Germans have a good word for it *machtbarkeit* which expresses the notion that you can shape events according to your wishes. That is basically wrong and becomes very clear if one understands how the human mind and the whole human civilization has developed. It has not been designed intelligently and men would have never been able to design it intelligently. Socialism is still an offspring of the erroneous conception that history can be shaped according to a pre-designed plan. Heillbroner, in his book, *Between Capitalism and Socialism,* has a phrase that expresses the fundamental idea of socialism which seems to me, intellectually, completely wrong: "It is a prime belief of socialism that man makes himself. Socialism can dispense itself of the need to formulate a conception of human nature by concentrating instead on the institutions by which that nature will be formed. In a word, human nature will be in the end what we want it to be." That leads me to argue that the difference between me and the socialists is not a moral difference but an intellectual difference. Different beliefs on what we have in our power to do and what we do not. That is very important because the socialists usually avoid discussion on this key issue by saying that we are dealing with an issue of value that lies outside science. It is not an issue of value. It is an intellectual issue and a very serious one: to determine what is beyond our control and what is not.

D.P.: Do you believe the majority of socialists are really interested in understanding the world and improving the explanatory power of their theories or are they motivated by the acquisition of power? It is very clear that an economist, for instance, is much more powerful in a centrally planned economy in comparison to the role he can play in a free enterprise system.

Professor Hayek: It is not possible to make a generalization. My next book is very much aimed at intellectual socialists and I hope that for them, the issue of power is a relatively minor issue. I am not sure but I do hope this is the case. However, when a socialist thinker becomes a politician, the desire to get to power overwhelms everything else. I am trying to get to the minds of socialist intellectuals and show them they are working on false ideas and concepts. It is not simply because we are dealing with different moral concepts but, most importantly, because they have an erroneous view of how society works and can work. I have tried to warn them: unless we correct the principles of our policies some very undesirable consequences, which most of the socialists would not accept, will follow.

D.P.: Many people think that Karl Marx made some contributions of interest to economic theory. According to Morishima, for instance, Marx and Walras should be honored together as the progenitors of the dynamic theory of economic equilibrium. It is of course well known, on the other hand, that most of the major predictions Marx made have failed completely. Yet I think that to explain how the system does not work is, in itself, an interesting contribution even if it is negative.

Professor Hayek: I agree that every error helps the advancement of knowledge and Marx's theories were certainly pure error. Aside from the failure of his predictions, which have refuted his system of thought, let me give you two examples that show how little understanding he had of social problems.

As I stated in my last book, Marx was completely unaware of the signal functions of prices. He was totally incapable of understanding how a selective evolution that knows no laws that determine its direction can produce a self-directing order. On the other hand, Marx did not understand that collectivistic economic planning leads inevitably to totalitarian tyranny, a thesis I developed in my *Road to Serfdom* and which has become increasingly recognized in the West.

D.P.: After having done research in the area of psychology, what is your opinion on the Freudian approach and its influence?

Professor Hayek: I consider that Freud is the greatest destroyer of civilization and culture with his basic aim of replacing culturally acquired habits by their innate instincts.

D.P.: To end this very interesting conversation, I would like to ask you what you consider to be Adam Smith's greatest contribution to economics.

Professor Hayek: I just came across a beautiful phrase in a book written by Simon Patten in 1899: "Smith was the last of the moralists and the first of the economists. Darwin was the last of the economists and the first of the biologists!"

Smith's greatest contribution is one that he himself partly disguised when he argued that the division of labor depends on the extent of the market. But when he gave the illustration of the division of labor, the famous pin factory, which is a deliberately created division, he misled his readers. Many people think that what Smith was illustrating was the organized division of labor inside a factory. What he really had in mind was the worldwide division of labor, that is to say, specialization between enterprises rather than within them. The division of labor is not an invention of the human mind, it is the evolution of a process.

Bibliography

Arrow, K., *Social Choice and Individual Values*, Yale, 1963.
Arrow, K. and Lind, R. "Uncertainty and the Evaluation of Public Investment Decisions," *American Economic Review*, 1970.
Erhard, L., Conference given when he received the *doctor honoris causa* degree at Universidad de los Andes, Bogotá, 1969.
Friedman, M., "Proposal for a negative income tax," *Capitalism and Freedom*, Chicago, 1962.
Friedman, M. and A. Schwartz, *A Monetary History of the United States*. Princeton, 1963.
Hayek, F.A., "Economics and Knowledge," *Economica*, 1936.
———, *The Pure Theory of Capital*, London, 1941.
———, *The Road to Serfdom*, London, 1944.
———, *Individualism and Economic Order*, London, 1948.
———, *The Counter-Revolution of Science*, London, 1952.
———, *The Sensory Order*, London, 1952.
———, (ed.), Capitalism and the Historians, London, 1954.
———, *The Constitution of Liberty*, London, 1960.
———, *Studies in Philosophy, Politics and Economics*, London, 1967.
———, "A Tiger by the Tail—The Keynesian Legacy of Inflation," Institute of Economic Affairs, London, 1973.
———, "The Pretence of Knowledge," Nobel Prize Lecture. Nobel Foundation, 1974.
———, "Full Employment at any Price?", IEA, London, 1975.
———, "Denationalization of Money," IEA, London, 1976.
———, *New Studies in Philosophy, Politics, Economics and the History of Ideas*, London, 1978.
———, *Law, Legislation and Liberty: Vol. I, Rules and Order*, London, 1973– *Vol. II, The Mirage of Social Justice*, London, 1976. *Vol. III, The Political Order of a Free Society*, London, 1979.
Hicks, J.R., *The Crisis in Keynesian Economics*, Oxford, 1974.
Keynes, J.M., *Collected Works*, Royal Economic Society, London, Macmillan, 1971–1979.
Kuhn, T.S., *The Structure of Scientific Revolutions*, Chicago, 1962.
Kresge, S. and Wenar, L. (eds). *Hayek on Hayek*, Chicago, 1994.
Morishima, M., *Marx's Economics*, Cambridge, 1973.
Machlup, F. (ed.), *Essays on Hayek*, London, 1977.
Myrdal, G., "Nobel Prize Lecture," Nobel Foundation, 1974.
Pizano, D., "A Conversation with Professor Jan Tinbergen," in this book.

A Conversation with
Professor John Hicks

The first time I heard of Professor John R. Hicks was in 1965, when I asked Jorge Franco, an economist friend of my father's, about his profession. Franco had studied at Harvard in the forties and had later traveled to Oxford in 1955 to pursue a graduate degree under the tutelage of Professor Hicks. "He is a very profound and erudite scholar," Franco told me. As I already mentioned, in 1977 I spent several months at Oxford, and therefore had the opportunity of visiting the Professor at his office at All Souls College. In his office he had magnificent editions of writings by all of the principal economists since the times of Adam Smith. He had the writings of Vilfredo Pareto in Italian. He also had books about some of the developing countries in Asia, Africa and the Caribbean, alongside International Monetary Fund and World Bank publications. He was following tendencies in global economics. When I presented him with the idea of my project he was enthusiastic. Beforehand I had sent him some of the questions I was interested in discussing and he was kind enough to answer them. However, he did not like improvisation and preferred to mull over his answers calmly. On one occasion he requested I grant him a week to prepare more coherent answers.

Sir John Hicks, 1904–1989, taught at the London School of Economics, Manchester University, and Johannesburg University and at Cambridge University. He was the Drummond Professor of political economy at Oxford until 1965. He wrote numerous articles and books, among these the following stand out: *The Theory of Wages* (1932), *Value and Capital* (1939), *Critical Essays in Monetary Theory* (1967), *A Theory of Economic History* (1969) and *Capital and Time* (1973). He was a member of the Nigerian Commission to Allocate Public Funds in 1950 and the Royal Commission on Taxes and Earnings in 1951. The Swedish Academy of Science awarded him a Nobel in 1972 for his important contributions to the discipline, in both microeconomic as in macroeconomic theory. This conversation took place in Oxford, England in June, 1977.

The Conversation

Diego Pizano: I would like to start by referring to your theory of wages since it is closely connected with one of the major economic debates of our times, the determinants of income distribution. I am aware that you are not happy nowadays with some of the assertions of the 1932 edition of *The Theory of Wages*, but people like Professor Schumpeter consider it a very fine work.

First of all, it would be interesting to know if you agree with Joan Robinson[7] and Maurice Dobb,[8] who sustain that economic theory lacks an income distribution theory. Dobb goes so far as to say that not even the most sophisticated Marxists have a good conceptual framework.

I suppose that a great deal of confusion has emerged from the fact that some authors do not clarify what the scope of the contribution of the economist is to such a complicated multifaceted question. I think economists cannot answer the normative question of what the distribution ought to be. However, I do believe they might be helpful in providing a workable theory that aims at explaining what economic factors account for the shape and the structure of the distribution. Perhaps, equally important, I would say that economists could shed light on the interactions between various macroeconomic objectives in such a way that policy makers can maneuver in a context of conflicts between policy goals.

This brief introduction brings me to the following question: to what extent do you regard your theory as part of normative or positive economics?

Would you consider the logically coherent version of the neoclassical economy in equilibrium as having causal significance, or only as a description of a possibly desirable state of affairs?

In a dynamic setting where there is both inflation and unemployment, would it be right to apply the marginal productivity theory?

Or, to the contrary, does it imply that you are comparing two equilibrium positions in a state of unbalance, and thus, could be misleading? In this connection would it be fruitful to integrate some

---

7. J. Robinson, "The Second Crisis in Economic Theory," *A.E.R.*, 1974.
8. M. Dobb, *Theories of Value and Distribution Since A. Smith*, Cambridge University Press, 1974.

aspects of your theory of wages to your own theory of the trade cycle? I think it would be interesting to explain what happens to the participation of the production factors in the different phases of the cycle. Another point I believe is worth analyzing would be the importance of monetary factors in the distribution of income. I have the impression that these could be important factors yet they seem to play a minor role in your theory.

On the other hand, I was wondering if you could comment on the following idea: As you know, there are two main approaches to the construction of an income distribution theory. One school of thought—Champernowne, for instance—assumes that income is the product of an infinite stochastic process acting multiplicatively. The other, Tinbergen for example, assumes that income is the product of a number of factors operating simultaneously. Don't you think that one could try to reconcile both approaches and integrate them? I am very surprised that I haven't come across an effort of this kind in the literature. What is your reaction to this line of thought?

Professor Hicks: In the second edition of my *Theory of Wages*, I have tried to explain what aspects of the original theory I reject as unsatisfactory. The first chapters on the working of the market form the part of the book with which I am nowadays least dissatisfied. I still claim that it is of permanent value to have shown that the labor market is, by nature, and quite independently of trade union organization, a very special kind of market that is likely to develop social as well as purely economic aspects. However, the original book has various drawbacks. It avoids the problem of capital: How is capital to be fitted into a static theory? This point is relevant for the analysis on the classification distinction that can be made between capital as a physical concept (machines) and capital as the fund concept. If we are making a static comparison, we ought to use the physical concept but if we are working, for example, in the field of development planning, I would not claim, myself, that there is much to be said for thinking in terms of marginal products.

You ask me whether I consider my theory as normative or positive. I would say it could be regarded as forming part of positive economics, I consider it to have causal significance, not in the sense of explaining the structure of the distribution at a point in time, but instead, in providing a framework that could serve as a guide to find out in what direction the various forces are working.

I have done some work on Ricardian Economics connected with this subject with Professor Hollander, which will appear soon in the *Quarterly Journal of Economics* (August, 1977). You also point out that it would be fruitful to integrate it with my own theory of the trade cycle. The problem is that I regard my contribution to the theory of wages as a long-run equilibrium theory, and my trade cycle theory looks to explain events taking place in the short and medium term. The approach of both works is very different. I took for granted what Harrod and Keynes had done and I am aware that an attempt has to be made to reconcile both of my works. A good part of my *Capital and Growth* (1965) could be regarded as an exploration in that direction.

D.P.: Another very interesting point I would like to discuss with you has to do with one of the numerous concepts you have introduced into economic theory and that is the elasticity of substitution. As you know, Joan Robinson and Champernowne introduced slightly different definitions that are equivalent to yours only if constant returns to scale are present. Now it seems clear to me that your definition and Robinson's are restricted to the case of linear homogeneous production functions, whereas Champernowne's is independent of the conditions of returns. If increasing returns are present, do you think your formula could be adapted to deal with the problem? Or would Arrow be right when he pointed out in his Nobel Prize Lecture that the issue of increasing returns is one of the major unresolved questions of economics?

Professor Hicks: My present feeling towards the elasticity of substitution is summarized in an article I published a few years ago in the *Oxford Economic Papers*.[9]

I was then concerned with the extension of the model to take into account at least three factors of production, to exhibit the character of substitution-complementarity relationships. As I suggest in my concluding remarks, Joan Robinson ought to have had the sole author's rights to the concept of elasticity of substitution. Mine should have been called something like "the elasticity of complementarity." Only in the two-production factor case would one be the reciprocal of the other.

---

9. J.R. Hicks, "Elasticity and Substitution Again: Substitutes and Complements," *O.E.P.*, November 1970.

I think the problem of linearity is important but there are other difficulties that could be even more important. The limitations of two factors cause greater difficulties and it is very misleading.

D.P.: As you have pointed out in one of your last books, *The Crisis in Keynesian Economics* (1975) future historians may well come to reckon the third quarter of this century as the age of Keynes. I consider that you could help economists in Latin America if you made some comments connected with the exegesis of Keynesian economics. This is clearly of some importance, given the fact that most Latin American governments have been influenced by the macroeconomic approach to the management of the economy in different degrees.

You were introduced to macroeconomics through the work of Hayek and trained in the general equilibrium tradition of Walras and Wicksell. However, you have said many times that you consider yourself as having been greatly influenced by Keynesian ideas. The obvious question would be: Do you really think Walras and Keynes can be reconciled and understood under the same framework?

I would think that your answer would include your invention of the IS-LM diagram which has had an enormous pedagogical value at universities all over the world, including Latin America. But is it a true representation of Keynes's thought? In your book you mention that the diagram was never intended as more than a representation of what appeared to be a central point of Keynes theory. You also point out that Keynes accepted it as such. But if one reads the correspondence you had with him,[10] it is not clear that the diagram did capture his innovations, particularly insofar as the notion of equilibrium and uncertainty generate important complications.

I want to argue that it is not possible to accommodate Keynes's theoretical contributions as a special case in the Walrasian tradition because of the following reasons:

(a) The epistemological foundations of Keynes's theories (not to be confused with the ideological foundations) were different from that of Walras. Keynes did not consider economics a natural science and, thus, he was not interested in providing a mechanistic explanation of human economic behavior like

---

10. J.M. Keynes. *Collected Works*, vol. XIV., Royal Economic Society, 1973.

Walras was. In this context, if there is a change in expectations, both the IS and the LM curves might shift simultaneously, and consequently the notion of equilibrium could be of little value, and

(b) Keynes did not believe in the possibility of constructing a deterministic model given the fact economic agents acted in a highly uncertain world. I am presently writing an essay showing that the connections between his *Treatise of Probability* and the axioms of the *General Theory* are illuminating yet, surprisingly, they have been overlooked. Keynes's discussion of subjective probabilities and the impossibility of measuring them in the real world are clearly connected to what in my view is his major contribution to economic theory: incorporating the Greek notion of tridimensional time by means of the role uncertainty plays in the model and having postulated the function of liquidity preference.

Your book on Keynesian economics gives the impression that you think Hayek might be becoming more relevant for the analysis of contemporary issues whereas the Keynes framework is loosing its explanatory power. Would this mean that the problems of predominant concern in contemporary economic and social policy in the developed nations are those that preoccupied Pigou—economic welfare and allocation of resources rather than the problems of unemployment and recession that worried Keynes? And, speaking of unemployment, would you agree with Hayek in stating that the Keynesian theory of unemployment was wrong and that the true case of unemployment is the distortion of relative prices that do not equate the demand for and the supply of labor in each sector of the economic system?

Professor Hicks: I should start by saying that I think that I need to change my name. *Value and Capital* was the work of a neoclassical economist, J.R. Hicks, now deceased; while *Capital and Time* (1973) and *A Theory of Economic History* (1969) are the work of John Hicks, a non-neoclassic, who is quite disrespectful towards his uncle.[11] It is important to note that the last two works belong

---

11. See J.R. Hicks, "Revival of Political Economy: The Old and the New," *Journal of the Economic Society of Australia and New Zealand*, September 1975.

together since they are both fruits of a historical approach. *Capital and Time* has the time system incorporated in an implicit way, but it can still be explained in terms that historians could understand. In *A Theory of Economic History* the time dimension is treated explicitly.

In *Capital and Time*, I do not assume that there would be a smooth convergence to equilibrium as a real neoclassic would have done. My suspicion is, instead, that the convergence may not be smooth at all, even under all the assumptions I made (I cut out money, monopolies, government and natural scarcities).

I have become very suspicious, not only of the production function, but also of the technology frontier. The distinction between substitutions along the frontier and changes in technology, which shift the frontier, I would now abandon.

Your remarks about the IS-LM diagram are of course, connected with the questions of time in economics. We represent time in our diagrams by a spatial coordinate; but that representation is never a complete representation. There is an obvious asymmetry between time and space. In space we can move any way, whereas time is irreversible; time just goes on and it never goes back.[12] Professor Georgescu has arrived at this simple principle by a cosmic way through the operation of the entropy law. I am very ignorant of the natural sciences and although I have dabbled in mathematics, my spiritual home is in the humanities and I have arrived at my views on time through the study of history. One of the main consequences of the asymmetry of time and space is that it gives rise to a great difference between past and future events. The knowledge we have, or can have, of the past is different in kind from what we can know of the future; for the latter, at best, is no more than knowledge of probabilities.

It is interesting to note that Carl Menger, in his theory of liquidity grasped—nearly one hundred years before Keynes—that the demand for money is only one aspect of a much more general kind of behavior. It is a matter of active provision against an uncertain future. Liquidity is certainly a problem of an economy in time.

I would say that Keynes's theory has one part that takes into account time explicitly, but it has another part that does not and is static. The part concerned with the marginal efficiency of capital

---

12. J.R. Hicks, "Evolution, Welfare and Time in Economics," *Essays in Honor of N. Georgescu-Roegen*, Toronto, 1976.

and with liquidity preference, is unquestionably in time. But there is another, the multiplier theory, which is out of time. It runs in terms of demand curves, supply and cost curves, just the old tools of equilibrium economics.

I agree with you when you say that the IS-LM diagram reduced the *General Theory* to equilibrium economics; it is not really in time. I have become conscious of how artificial this procedure was. Growth Theory, since Von Neumann, has been the scene of a tremendous comeback of equilibrism. Theorists trying to get one step ahead of Keynes slipped behind him. What made this possible was the discovery of the steady state.

Your remarks about the links between Keynes's theory of probability and his *General Theory* seem to be relevant, and I would say that it could be a very promising line of research. It is because I want to make economics more human that I want to make it more time conscious. It is the new things that humanity has discovered that make history exciting. And it is only the new things that may be found in the future, before humanity blows itself up, or settles down to some ghastly equilibrium, that make a future worth praying for.

On the question of the applicability of the Keynesian theory of unemployment to contemporary issues, I would not say that the theory is wrong, but rather that it is incomplete. Keynes was concerned with involuntary unemployment, a kind of unemployment due to lack of effective demand. But that is not the only cause. It would be a misuse of terms to speak of voluntary unemployment. Thus, I think that Keynes's distinction was not clear. As soon as trade unions demand a particular level of wages we are liable to get unemployment for reasons Keynes would call "voluntary:" distortions, rigidities, etc.

D.P.: Hayek's goes on to suggest[13] that the first step in order to remedy the problem of stagflation is to stop the rate of increase in the quantity of money. For him, the primary aim of economic policy should be stability in the value of money, and not full unemployment. I suppose you don't agree with him since you have rejected the monetarist explanation in your 1974 article in *Lloyds Bank Review*. I have two comments about your position:

---

13. F.A. Hayek, "Full Employment At Any Price?" *IEA*, London, 1975.

1) Do you think an income policy could work, or would you agree with Hayek in that it would only conceal the effects of continuing inflation but ultimately and inevitably produce a totalitarian system?
2) To what extent would Harry Johnson[14] be right in asserting that you failed to notice the difference in policy constraints between a fixed and a floating exchange rate system, and between a stable and an inflationary outside world?

Professor Hicks: Regarding your question concerning the monetarist explanation, I would like to answer in the following way. I have said that the monetarist view is incomplete, not totally wrong. I can think of three main reasons for the acceleration of prices in the industrial world in recent years: (i) There is no doubt that the raw material crisis of 1972–73 had a major effect in increasing the rise in consumer prices, (ii) The general floating of currencies may well have worked the same way. (iii) Even before the floating, and before the raw material crisis, the rate of inflation in consumer prices tended to increase.

It is clear to me that over the last twenty years, there has been underlying inflationary pressure that the floating and the raw material crisis have indeed aggravated. But the important thing to notice is that the underlying pressure cannot be easily explained by reference to the theory, that it is associated with an external cause, namely the situation of the balance of payments in the United States, nor is it possible to associate it with just an increase in the quantity of money.

D.P.: The problem of economic fluctuations and instability is a matter of public concern, and still remains a subject of widespread analysis. It is evident that a better understanding on the part of decision makers of the causes of cyclic behavior is critical to the formulation of effective stabilization policies.

Several categorizations of business cycle theories are currently available in the economic literature (Gordon, 1961; Haberler, 1964; Mass 1975). However, the essential common characteristic these models share is that they rely upon fluctuations in fixed capital

---

14. H. Johnson, "What Is Right with Monetarism?" *Lloyds Bank Review*, April 1976.

investments to explain business cycle behavior. I think this is not surprising if one takes into account that Keynes himself put forward the idea that the essential character of the trade cycle is mainly due to the way in which the marginal efficiency of capital fluctuates.

It would be highly interesting if you could make some remarks on the following propositions: (i) Capital investment theories seem to be largely inadequate for explaining short term business cycle behavior, although they may provide useful insights into causes of medium term cycles.

As Abramovitz has pointed out, fixed capital investment cannot be the intrinsic cause of short-term cycles because of the long delays in fixed capital construction and depreciation. (ii) All of the main theories (Harrod, Hicks, Goodwin and Kaldor) explain the fluctuations of demand by means of a single mechanism. In effect, all fluctuations are treated alike and the differences are given little emphasis. In the light of recent experiences in the western world, would you agree that it is perhaps too ambitious to seek a monistic explanation of fluctuations in income? (iii) Would you reconstruct your own cycle theory along the lines you suggested in your book about the crisis in Keynesian economics? (iv) Your model, like Harrod's, is characterized by extreme instability. Do you think that the record of postwar growth in industrial countries contradicts the essence of your theory? Finally have major depressions been produced by a variety of different types of shocks and not by a regular cycle-producing mechanism?

Professor Hicks: The acceleration theory, deeply influenced by Keynes, was the basis for the construction of my trade cycle model, but I think it was too elaborate a version. I have formulated my new position in a recent publication.[15] I was careful to leave a place for monetary influences but the greater part of the model neglects money and pays little attention to prices.

In its simplest form, the accelerator model is very violent: too violent, indeed, to make sense. If saving (S) is geared to output (Y), but investment to the rate of change of output (cg), saving equals investment gives $SY = cg\ Y$; so $S = cg$ (Harrod's equation) is a condition of equilibrium. I was unhappy with this fact because, as you were saying, it is an equilibrium that is inherently unstable.

---

15. J.R. Hicks, *Economic Perspectives: Further Essays on Money and Growth*, London, 1977.

There is nothing in the simple model which would stop downward fluctuation, short of complete collapse. Thus if the accelerator model was to fit the facts it had to be modified or cooled. That is why I introduced two coolants which amount to the introduction of lags, given the fact it is an instantaneous adjustment that is so explosive. My other coolant was autonomous investment. I allowed for the existence of investment, which is relatively independent of current output, whether long-range or not. This was done again with an eye on historical application.

When you ask whether the major depressions have been produced by a variety of different types of shocks, I would agree with that statement. It is precisely the introduction of autonomous investment, which allows me to introduce two kinds that need to be distinguished. One is that which springs from invention. The other is public investment, the amount of which must surely be regarded variable, at least to some extent, as a matter of policy. But these coolants are not the only ones. Two others, which I did not use in my book must be now mentioned. One is non-linearity, that is the rejection of the Harrodian proportionality between output and consumption. On the other hand, and perhaps more importantly, there is a qualification that must be introduced into the accelerator itself. Why should investment be geared to the rate of change of current output, even with a lag? That will only make sense if a rise in output requires an increase in capacity. The elasticity of capacity must be emphasized.

It must however be admitted that when the model is modified in these latter ways, it changes its character. It ceases to be a mathematical model, like one that might conceivably be used as an econometric hypothesis. Mathematics (or some parts of it) have provided some illuminating exercises; but they cannot be applied in their current form.

D.P: I wonder if you could illuminate us a little in presenting a picture of the present state of the British economy. I am aware that it is difficult to summarize and assess the record since the Second World War, but the British experience is highly relevant for countries like Colombia, that consider it worthwhile to learn from the experience of others.

Compared to other industrial nations, the economic performance of Britain since the war has not been very encouraging. Its share in the world trade of manufacturing has fallen by more than half, and so has the dollar value of the pound. Output per head is rather low when compared to France or West Germany. What are the predominant causes of what has been called the decline and fall of Britain? (a) Technological, in the sense that techniques are obsolete by American standards? (b) Psychological, in the sense that people prefer leisure to work? (c) Social, in the sense that the educational system is not geared towards economic growth? (d) Institutional, in the sense that economic policy has not been appropriate and the public sector has increased beyond its optimum size? In the case of the steel industry, for example, which suffered nationalization, denationalization and then re-nationalization, is it not a symptom of lack of stability in the government's policy? (e) Ecological, in the sense that various limits to growth are now operating?

Professor Hicks: A quick way of defining my position on this issue would be to say that I largely agree with W. Eltis[16] when he writes about the failure of the Keynesian conventional wisdom and the debate with Lord Kahn of Cambridge University.

British economic policy of the last twenty-five years destroyed the profitability of industry; the government appropriated a very large part of national income and I would say the size of the public sector went beyond any definition of optimum size. The attitude towards the irrelevance of deficits and the indifference towards inflation have had very adverse effects.

D.P.: Can it be said that one of the causes of the economic slow-down was the lack of scientific progress? It is very striking and paradoxical for me to see that Britain is still a world leader in various scientific areas (molecular biology, for instance) and in spite of this, its techniques are described as obsolete. Could it be that scientific research is not geared towards economic growth or that there is a long delay between a scientific discovery and its application in industry?

Professor Hicks: I do not pretend to know anything about this point, but let me tell you that I was much impressed by the history of the Imperial Chemical Industry. Germany had a lead in this field

---

16. W. Eltis, "The Failure of Keynesian Conventional Wisdom," *Lloyds Bank Review*, 1976.

since they took over in 1914 when they proposed a joint venture to the British firm involved in this area of production. But it was a highly complicated business and a divorce had to be planned in a neutral country, Holland. In the twenties the Germans continued to be leaders, but in the fifties the situation changed. The British firm was transformed and a wide new range of products was introduced. A very good record emerged and the competitiveness of this firm was very good by international standards. Now, this kind of development hasn't continued. I think it is due to the government's economic policy. If the delay you point out is longer than in the other countries, the explanation must have something to do with the government's economic policy, which destroyed the incentives to invest and to increase efficiency by adopting better techniques of production.

D.P.: When one looks at the presidential addresses delivered to the Royal Economic Society and the American Economic Association over the last years one has the impression, almost inevitably, that there seems to be a deep dissatisfaction with the current state of economic knowledge. Do you think that there is a set of contemporary events that cannot easily be accommodated within traditional categories? In other words, do you find a large gap exists between the theoretical constructions and the real world?

Professor Hicks: Well, I think that is a very difficult question to answer. What I can say is that the industrial world made a very serious mistake during the sixties when it assumed that the supply of primary products was elastic and that we could plan an expanding universe without having to take into account any important constraints. I am writing a book that addresses these issues and I expect it to be published next summer.[17]

The outstanding feature of the evolution of the world economic system during the last decades has been a lack of balance between the supply of industrial products and that of primary products. The terms of trade, as we all know, have evolved in the last years in favor of the latter. This situation has created expectations in many countries all over the world. But unless it is possible to develop forms of industry that are not dependent on primary products,

---

17. This was ultimately published under the title *Economic Perspectives: Further Essays on Money and Growth*, New York, 1977.

the attempt to industrialize the developing countries will make the competition for scarce resources more acute. Even if we were to imagine a world government with the power and the means to industrialize the whole world, it would soon face the problem of not being able to do so without a big cut in the standard of living of the rich countries and these countries would resist such a cut.

D.P.: I think one could logically derive two corollaries from your statement: (i) The pattern of the international income distribution cannot easily be changed, (ii) Only a few developing countries will be able to reach a high level of industrialization unless there is a technological breakthrough that amplifies raw material sources significantly. On the other hand, it is true that the terms of trade have improved for the primary producing countries. But I do not think that a swing in the terms of trade in favor of the primary producers is likely to last for long, since the industrial countries will resist any compression of their standard of living through a cost-induced inflation of industrial prices.

Professor Hicks: Yes, I certainly believe that only a few countries will be able to industrialize. I have always been interested in the comparative economic history of Australia and Argentina. The analysis of the experiences of these two countries should serve as a lesson to other countries. Both countries are fairly similar insofar as racial origins and natural resources are concerned. In both cases, you find big cities and a strong opposition of interests between the industrial and the agricultural sectors. But Argentina's record of development is not as good as Australia's. Argentina was growing well until the conflict between sectors coupled with an economic policy that discriminated against agriculture led to stagnation. In such circumstances, there is an extraordinary tendency to cut one's throat. I don't know what the situation is like in Colombia.

D.P.: Colombia adopted the import substitution strategy after the Great Depression. As a result, an industrial sector emerged. Nevertheless, this had a price in terms of the discrimination against agriculture, insufficient generation of employment, balance of payment difficulties and exponential growth of cities. The strategic issue regarding the choice of techniques did not receive very much attention and the question of the optimal tariff structure was not tackled adequately based on macroeconomic criteria.

Professor Hicks: I think that economists have been placing too much stress on the question of the appropriate degree of capital or labor-intensiveness. I think we should better start thinking in terms of the degree of fuel intensity or primary product intensity of production.

D.P.: From what you have just said, it seems that you would agree in recommending economists to take natural resources into account in their models since the law of entropy implies an irrevocable process of transformation of energy.

Professor Hicks: I think that is true. But one should distinguish between the physical limits established by the scientists and the economic effects. The latter tend to become apparent much earlier than the former, as in the time of Jevons and the coal question of the 1860s.

One should never forget that the fundamental significance of industrialization is the substitution of fossil fuels for human energy. The mysterious thing we call capital has less to do with the process of economic growth in comparison with the sources of energy.

D.P.: I think the problem of the future of the planet's economic growth is unpredictable since the future course of technological evolution cannot be predicted beforehand. It is obvious that new inventions cannot have pre-existence. Consequently, there is no reliable method for undertaking long term economic forecasts such as those put forward by groups such as the Club of Rome.

Professor Hicks: I agree with you that economists cannot predict the future course of human history.

D.P.: In this context, would you agree with Schumpeter in the sense that economists should concentrate their research efforts on providing an explanation of historical events?

Professor Hicks: I think that is an important aspect of the economist's work, but it is important to try to work a bit into the future as well. Economists can sometimes anticipate some of the consequences of adopting particular economic strategies and policies.

D.P.: With reference to this question about the future, would you agree with Keynes when he pointed out that the long run is for undergraduates and that in the long run we are all dead?

Professor Hicks: I must say that was a very dangerous and irresponsible remark.

D.P.: Turning to another topic, I would like to know your opinion on the question of the optimum degree of planning. Do you think that the tendency of different economic systems to converge has shed light upon the central question of how much planning is necessary and in what areas?

Professor Hicks: I think that is a question one cannot answer in the abstract. Ambitious planning requires a large bureaucracy and this might lead to inefficiency and corruption. As you were telling me, there seems to be a great deal of urban unemployment and underemployment in Colombia. I think that countries that have to face this serious problem should concentrate their efforts on reducing it.

D.P.: But do you think that it is possible and plausible to reduce unemployment only through the free operation of market forces?

Professor Hicks: Well, it is a difficult question to answer since very few countries have had a really free market. On the other hand, one musts remember that restrictions like import licenses do not encourage employment in all cases.

D.P.: I would like to ask you a question of a different character. Would you agree with Keynes when he asserts that the world is ruled by the ideas of economists and political philosophers?

Professor Hicks: I do not agree. I think economists can be useful but they should not try to be too ambitious.

Bibliography

W. Baumol, "John R. Hicks Contribution to Economics," *Swedish Journal of Economics*, 74, 1972.

O.F. Hamouda, *John R. Hicks, The Economist's Economist*. Oxford, Blackwell, 1993.

J.R. Hicks, *The Theory of Wages*. London, Macmillan, 1932.

———, *Value and Capital*, Oxford, Clarendon Press, 1939.

———, *Capital and Growth*, Oxford, Clarendon Press, 1965.

———, *Critical Essays in Monetary Theory*, Oxford University Press, 1967.

———, *A Theory of Economic History*. Oxford University Press, 1969.

———, "*Nobel Prize Lecture*," Nobel Foundation, 1973.

———, *The Crisis in Keynesian Economics*. New York, 1974.

———, *Economic Perspectives*. Oxford University Press, 1976.

J.A. Kregel (ed.), *Recollections of Eminent Economists*. Macmillan, 1988.

S. Pressman, *Fifty Major Economists*. Second Edition, Routledge, 2006.

A Conversation with
Professor Nicholas Kaldor

This distinguished Professor was born in Budapest in 1908. He studied at the same school as the famous Professor John Von Neumann, and in fact, they met years later in Berlin. He studied at the London School of Economics where he met Professors Hicks and Hayek. In 1939 he met Keynes, and, a few years later, he moved to Cambridge where he became a part of a circle of Professors teaching there. He taught many students of distinction, among these, two winners of the Nobel Prize in Economics: Amartya Sen and Leonid Hurwicz. Other outstanding students of his were Jadgwish Bhagwatti, one of the great international trade theorists and Manmohan Singh, who is currently the Prime Minister of India.

I had the opportunity to attend his conferences on the theory of growth and conversed with him several times during my time at Cambridge (1972–74). He was determined to improve the economic performance of both industrialized as well as developing nations.

Lord Nicholas Kaldor (1908–1986) was, for many years, a Fellow at King's College and Professor of Economics at Cambridge University. His publications include: *An Expenditure Tax* (1955), *Essays on Value and Distribution* (1960), *Essays an Economic Stability and Growth* (1960), *Essays on Economic Policy*, vol. I & vol. II (1964), *Further Essays on Economic Theory* (1978), and *Further Essays on Applied Economics* (1978). He contributed to Sir William Beveridge's celebrated research: *Full Employment in a Free Society*. Between 1947 and 1949 he was the Director of the UN Research Commission for Europe. He was a member of the Royal Commission on Taxes from 1951 until 1955. He acted as an economic consultant to the governments of India, Ceylon (now Sri Lanka), Ghana, Mexico and Turkey, advising on the reform of their tax systems. He was in contact with several economists working in Latin America, such as Professor Lauchlin Currie from Colombia and Professor Celso Furtado from Brazil. In 1975 he was elected President of the Royal Economic Society. He is considered to be one of the great Keynesian economists of the XXth century. This conversation took place at his home in Cambridge, England during the month of August 1977.

The Conversation

Diego Pizano: Many people, including professional economists,[18] regard economic theory as an extremely abstruse and complex subject with little relation to the world of observation and experience. At the same time, economics is described as a social science, concerned with the study of one important aspect of human society. Economic theory, therefore, should be able to contribute to our understanding of developed and underdeveloped countries. I would like to hear your views on two related questions before I proceed to discuss specific points related to your contributions to economic theory:

(a) Economists have been trying to apply scientific methods of analysis to the economic aspects of society's activities. Do you think that advances in the past forty years have made them more and not less capable of illuminating social questions?

(b) What would be your definition of the scope of economic theory: Is it concerned with theories on the forces that govern demand and supply in business life (Marshall), or with the allocation of scarce resources about competing ends (Robbins), or with the determinants of income distribution (Ricardo), or with how the economy works at the macro level (Keynes)?

Professor Kaldor: The logical system of equilibrium economics,[19] which is the prevailing theory of value in most universities of the Western world, has become a major obstacle to the development of economics as a science. The American economists of the Mathematical School of the post-war generation have been

---

18. Lauchlin Currie, *La enseñanza de la economía*, Bogotá, 1962.
19. General Equilibrium Systems (GES) were initially developed by L. Walras in the last century, for the purpose of capturing a characteristic of the structure of the economy, which was the interdependence of the prices of all goods. This contrasts with the method of partial equilibrium adopted by A Marshall, who, in analysing the economics of a good, supposes that the prices of all others remain constant (*caeteris paribus*). The system of general equilibrium is normally represented by a set of simultaneous equations that need to be solved in order to find the prices of all supplies and products of the economy.

responsible for the clarification of the kind of postulates required to establish its conclusions and their precise implications.

Now, to answer your first question, I would say that the results of this great abstract exercise have made the theory a less usable tool than it was thought to have been in its early and crude state. There has not been great progress in traditional economic theory over the last decades.[20] The post-war era has been a period of the "counter-reformation" of economics. After the thirties, when the whole traditional theory came under attack as the result of the appearance of Keynesian economics and the theories of imperfect competition, most of the traditional economists decided to eliminate the important effects of this intellectual breakthrough by refining the system of equilibrium economics to an extreme.

Regarding the scope of economic theory, I would say that the essence of economics should not be regarded as an allocation problem. The essential complementarity between different factors of production such as capital and labor, or different economic sectors, such as the primary, secondary and tertiary, is far more important than the substitution aspect stressed by economists such as Marshall and Robbins.

D.P.: In other words, you find that the concept of the elasticity of substitution[21] is not relevant at all?

Professor Kaldor: The principle of substitution is the most important one of neoclassical economics. Yet I think that it is precisely this principle that makes equilibrium theory static and lifeless. It aims at "explaining" a system of market clearing prices that are the resultant of various economic interactions; therefore it cannot deal with the idea of prices acting as a system that generates a series of signals that act as incentive to change.[22]

---

20. By traditional economic theory Professor Kaldor means the neoclassical school, not the Keynesian one.
21. The elasticity of substitution is defined as the proportional change in the technical marginal rate of substitution. If the elasticity of substitution is equal to zero, then we have a production function with fixed coefficients (there is no possibility of substituting capital for work).
22. Kaldor is affirming that what is interesting about the price system is that it induces changes in the economic structure (what is called the creative function of the market), and he is not interested in the allocation function that leads to a situation that tends to maintain itself (definition of equilibrium in neoclassical theory).

D.P.: I do not know to what extent you are implying that the deductive path economic theory has followed is the wrong one. If you are complaining against the degree of abstraction of mainstream economics, couldn't one say that unorthodox theories such as Sraffa's, Robinson's and yours are equally abstract?

Professor Kaldor: It is my impression that abstract mathematical models lead nowhere and it is becoming increasingly recognized that econometrics do not lead anywhere either. The development of refined methods of statistical inference cannot serve the function of providing a realistic framework for how the economy works. However, I must make it clear from the outset that my fundamental criticism to the theory of general equilibrium is not that it is abstract. All scientific disciplines are abstract given the fact there can be no analysis without abstraction. The trouble is that General Equilibrium Systems (GES) start from the wrong kind of abstractions and, as a consequence they give a wrong picture of how the economy really works.

D.P.: Some of the people that have been involved in the capital theory controversy between Cambridge and MIT give the impression that the weakest point in neoclassical theory is the possibility of re-switching of techniques.[23] However, I have the impression that other assumptions, such as perfect foresight and constant returns to scale, could be much more important from the empirical and logical point of view, in the sense that they restrict the explanatory power of GES systems more than any other assumption.

Professor Kaldor: I am aware of the fact that some of my Cambridge colleagues believe that there is a single logical objection (the difficulty of measuring the quantity of capital) which makes neoclassical theory misleading. But I think that there are more important objections. Among these, the existence or non-linearities in the production function of increasing returns to scale, which are wholly excluded by the axiomatic framework of neoclassical theory,

---

23. This problem refers to the difficulty of specifying a unique association between the incremental capital-product relation and the relative prices of the factors. This has been a central topic in the Cambridge–MIT debates and is connected to the discussion about the measuring of capital and the impact of interest rates in determining the grade of mechanization of the techniques used in productive processes.

has very far-reaching effects. Nobody has been able to incorporate them within GES since they have destructive consequences.

Regarding the issue of linearity I want to say that it is interesting to note that Professor Kantorovich (Russian Nobel Prize winner) has been working for many years on the subject of optimal planning. He points out in some of his recent essays[24] that the necessary and sufficient condition for an optimal plan is the existence of a system of shadow prices found as a solution of the dual of a linear programming problem.[25] He is aware of the problem of non-convexities due to the existence of increasing returns to scale and recently he has developed a multi-period model of a national economic plan designed for optimization over time and taking into account non-linearities. What is surprising is that Kantorovich starts from the Marxian framework of reproduction and ends up close to the Walrasian model.

I cannot see how he manages to relax the assumption of linearity.

D.P: His procedure consists in breaking down non-linear cost functions into linear segments and treating each segment as a separate ingredient of the plan.

Professor Kaldor: The procedure you describe seems more interesting than the American way of relaxing linearity, which consists of assuming that cost curves are U-shaped and that beyond a certain scale plan one encounters increasing costs. However, that is not what I call relaxing linearity. When one relaxes the assumption of linearity, the very notion of general equilibrium collapses since the forces[26] making for continuous changes become endogenous and are no longer treated as external shocks that move the equilibrium position of the system as the neoclassicals assume.

---

24. L.V. Kantorovich, *Essays in Optimal Planning*, Oxford, 1977,
25. Kantorovich used the analysis of activities which applies the techniques of lineal programming to GES. Professor Kantorovich received the Nobel Prize in 1975 jointly with Professor Koopmans for his contributions in this area. See T. Koopmans, *Activity Analysis of Production and Allocation*, New York, 1951.
26. The existence of increasing returns to scale changes the behavior of economic agents, particularly that of producers, who need to increase the scale of their plant in order to maximize their profits. By increasing their market share they reach a situation of imperfect competition, or oligopoly, in which the concept of a unique and stable equilibrium loses validity.

D.P.: To what extent do the paths opened by the theories of imperfect competition (Robinson, Chamberlain) developed in the thirties overcome some of the difficulties you have mentioned? I am skeptical about Joan Robinson's theory, since she omits the case of oligopoly, criticism she accepted in a discussion we had recently.[27]

Professor Kaldor: Those theories you mention have never been integrated within GES since they were destructive. These doctrines were gradually forgotten and the more recent formulations ignore their existence. With reference to Joan Robinson's book I wrote a review many years ago[28] stating that her work constituted a significant advance in economic theory; however, she neglects the problems of duopoly and that is, of course, an important weakness of that work.

D.P: There is now a growing literature on duopoly theory[29] which is still in its infancy but has provided new vistas on the problem.

Professor Kaldor: There is no single theory of duopoly which explains, in a realistic way, how prices are determined in industry. Nobody has a clear idea of how competition works in circumstances where each producer faces a limited market in regards to sales and yet, a highly competitive market in regards to prices.

D.P.: I am of the opinion that Von Neumann's theory of games and subsequent developments of bargaining theory have put oligopoly theory in a very interesting perspective which needs to be exploited much further.

Professor Kaldor: Nobody has been able to show that any proposition of game theory has any relevance to, let us say, the determination of motorcar prices in the United States. The link has not been established yet at the empirical level. For the reasons I have discussed, and which are expanded in two recent papers,[30]

---

27. D. Pizano, "A Conversation with Professor Joan Robinson," in this book.
28. N. Kaldor, "Mrs. Robinson's 'Economics of Imperfect Competition,'" *Economica*, August 1934.
29. See for instance, Cyert, R.M. and de Groot, M.H: "An Analysis of Cooperation and Learning in a Duopoly Context," *American Economic Review*, 1973, 63.
30. N. Kaldor, "The Irrelevance of Equilibrium Economics," *Economic Journal*, Dec. 1972; N. Kaldor, "What is wrong with Economic Theory?", *Quarterly Journal of Economics*, August 1975.

I do not think GES provides the right sort of tool to approach a decentralized economic system.

D.P.: But wouldn't you consider that GES could be regarded as a heuristic device in the sense that one has to begin with easy cases? Let's remember that Newton began his theoretical work in celestial dynamics by taking the planets to be petit-masses. Having solved the problem in this case he proceeded to consider them as spheres of uniform density and later oblate spheres of non-uniform densities. I am not asserting economics should follow the method of celestial mechanics (which was Walras's dream), but if we want a description of the steady state or general equilibrium of the whole economic system it seems reasonable to begin with a fictitious case in which we can at least expect answers. Then we can proceed to relax assumptions in order to face more complicated cases.

Professor Kaldor: The trouble is that in the case of GES you have to maintain the whole set of abstractions. If you relax any one of the key axioms the whole structure collapses. As I stated, the system cannot survive if one relaxes the abstraction of linearity, for instance.

D.P.: I remember that Professor Hahn pointed out in his inaugural lecture[31] that it was possible to incorporate increasing returns to scale in the general equilibrium framework under certain conditions.

Professor Kaldor: Hahn's position does not make any sense whatsoever; he simply stated that it is possible to introduce economies of scale when they do not matter because they are not relevant. This is absolute nonsense. No one has been able to show how to take into account increasing returns when they are effective.

D.P.: I was wondering how important are economies of scale from an empirical point of view. Two studies come to mind in this moment. The first one is Denison's well-known study on "Why growth rates differ."[32] The second one is Pratten's study on economies of

---

31. F. Hahn, "An Inaugural Lecture," Cambridge 1973. When a scholar becomes a Professor, he must then prepare a lecture to inaugurate his professorship. The title of full "Professor" is only granted to the most outstanding scholars.
32. E. Denison, *Why Growth Rates Differ*, Brookings Institute, 1967.

scale in the British Manufacturing Industry.[33] They both conclude that increasing returns to scale are important as sources of growth; however, it is not clear how they separate economies of scale from learning by doing and technical progress.

Professor Kaldor: At the empirical level, one can say, without doubt, that in industry increasing returns dominate the picture. Provided that the technical problems of construction can be solved, an increase in size is bound to bring further cost reductions since capacity is bound to increase faster than construction costs. Thus, it is clear that plant costs per unit of output necessarily decrease with size in activities such as steel plants, chemical plants or electricity generators. There is a rapidly growing volume of empirical facts which makes the neglect of economies of scale by theoreticians an intellectual scandal. In addition to the study by Pratten, which you mentioned, let me say that among other studies the Manual of the O.E.C.D. Development Centre on Industrial Projects contains an Annex with evidence of very large scale economies in almost every major manufacturing sector.

In reference to the empirical distinction between increasing returns and technical progress I agree with your statement. In a paper I published in the *Oxford Economic Papers*[34] I have argued that, since there is no way to distinguish one from the other, it is meaningless to assert that a particular source of growth is due to either of them.

D.P.: How would you connect this debate on GES and their relevance with another debate that is being carried out in Latin American countries and the United States, which is concerned with the potentials and limitations of economic planning? It is my impression that the people who have been actively involved in developing GES are inclined to believe in the invisible hand, whereas the people who recognize the failures and flaws you have pointed out are advocating for a greater degree of economic planning.

Professor Kaldor: I think it is not a question of failures or flaws. They do exist of course, but the main question is to determine

---

33. C.F. Pratten, *Economies of Scale in Manufacturing Industry*, Cambridge University Press, 1971.
34. N. Kaldor, "Increasing Returns and Technical Progress: A Comment on Professor Hick's Article," *Oxford Economic Papers*, February 1961.

how the economic system works. I think that the Walrasian model does not illuminate us on the nature and the manner in which economic forces operate. Consequently, we need to construct a different theoretical framework with a greater interpretative value of reality; from this effort you cannot assert that a particular position has to follow necessarily with regards to the question of economic planning.

D.P.: Do you intend to say that one cannot establish policy conclusions out of these theoretical efforts?

Professor Kaldor: Sometimes yes, sometimes no, one cannot know a priori. Thinking in terms of the two sector model I am working on, I can say that one of my main conclusions up to now is that it is a good thing to stabilize raw material prices by means of buffer stocks since this is the true constraint on the development of the world economy and not capital and labor. Capital is automatically created if you increase industrial production. Labor is available in very large quantities in today's world. Moreover, there is never an optimal allocation of labor. Even if all labor is employed, one can always increase productivity by redistributing that labor. And then you cannot distinguish between an increase in the labor supply and an increase in the efficiency of labor via redistribution. The neoclassicals assume one cannot get increased labor efficiency by this procedure and thus, the only alternative to increase production in the short run is to increase the supply of labor. In reality this is not so. The distinction between changes in the quantity of resources and changes in the efficiency with which they are used becomes a questionable one. There is never a Pareto-optimal allocation of resources. There can never be one because the world is in a state of disequilibrium; new technologies keep appearing and it is not sensible to assume a timeless, steady state.

D.P.: I will make some comments on your two-sector model, but let me say before that, even if it does not make sense, that we will assume that an optimal allocation of resources exists in a dynamic context. The concept of opportunity cost seems reasonable to me. I think it is a concept that should be taken into account when one is planning a tariff structure or an export promotion strategy in a less developed country.

Professor Kaldor: Well, I would accept that there are some legitimate uses of the concept of opportunity cost and it is natural that in my battle against GES I have concentrated on the illegitimate ones. Economics can only be seen as a medium for the "allocation of scarce means between alternative uses" in the consideration of short run problems where the framework of social organization and the distribution of available resources can be treated as given as a heritage of the past, and current decisions on future developments have no impact whatsoever.

Economic theory went astray when theoreticians focused their attention on the allocative functions of markets to the exclusion of their creative functions, which are far more important since they serve as an instrument for transmitting economic changes.

D.P.: If traditional economic theory (and that applies to other schools of thought as well) cannot make non-trivial predictions concerned with economic life I would ask: Is economic planning possible? Some people have postulated "laws" in economic life such as Pareto's law of unchangeable inequality of income, Denison's law of constant private saving ratio, Colin Clark's law of a 25 percent ceiling on government expenditure and taxation, Marx's law of the falling rate of profit, Keynes's consumption function which he assumed to be based upon a psychological law, etc. However, I am of the opinion that it is not possible to make large scale forecasts about economic events because economic change is influenced in a very significant degree by changes in knowledge, and future knowledge cannot be gained before its time. I think that one of the reasons that explain the failure of planning in Latin American countries is due to lack of awareness of the obstacles for large-scale predictions. Planners are certainly not omniscient minds and after all, who is going to plan the planners?

In short, I have the impression that your attack on GES could lead one to think that the invisible hand does not guarantee an optimum allocation of resources and consequently, that the only answer is central planning. But, parallel to the failures of the market, one can point out failures of the visible hand which in certain cases can be equally or even more important.

Professor Kaldor: Indicative planning of the Latin American type has been, certainly, a failure. But I consider that a well-conceived and a well-planned government intervention can accelerate economic developments. If policy instruments are well synchronized, different combinations of macroeconomic goals can be approached with a certain degree of rationality.

D.P.: I was wondering to what extent growth theories can provide useful guidelines to government action. I might perhaps pursue this line of thought a little by making a few comments on your own theories of growth.[35] First of all, why is it that you assume full employment and long-run equilibrium in your model if you consider that the world is in a state of profound disequilibrium?

Professor Kaldor: I agree that those are unrealistic axioms to make; however, they are necessary conditions for a one-sector model.

D.P.: Why do you assume that the labor force grows at a constant rate? Why is it that theoretical demographers and theoretical economists have not made a combined effort to introduce accumulated experience on the impact of the growth of population on economic growth and vice versa? There is now a rapidly expanding literature on the dynamics of population growth. Professor Coale of Princeton University,[36] for instance has written a book on the growth and structures of human populations using as the basic premise the weak endogenicity theorem of Alvaro Lopez-Toro (who was a member of the economics faculty, Universidad de los Andes, Bogotá).[37] It is surprising to me that growth theorists neglect this type of contribution.

Professor Kaldor: I do agree that most growth theorists treat demographic phenomena as exogenous. However, I did say that population growth depends on economic growth, but then one reaches a stage where the relationship breaks down and there is no further association between the two variables. I think it was not a bad approximation for Europe except for migration.

D.P.: A striking aspect of your model is that the capital-output ratio is not influenced by the rate of profit as reflected in the equation

---

35. I am referring to models constructed during the fifties. See N. Kaldor, "A Model of Economic Growth," *Economic Journal*, 1957, pp. 591–624.
36. A. Coale, *The Growth and Structure of Human Populations*, Princeton, 1972.
37. A. López Toro, "Problems in Stable Population Theory," Princeton, 1961; "Asymptotic Properties of a Human Age Distribution Under a Continuous Net Fertility Function," *Demography*, 1967.

$S=I/Y$;[38] this would imply, of course, that in the choice between less and more mechanized techniques, the rate of profit does not play any role whatsoever and this seems to be unrealistic.

Professor Kaldor: I assume the inverse relation, that is to say, that the higher the expected rate of profit is, the higher the incentive is for entrepreneurs to adopt a more labor saving technique. This is, of course, in conflict with the neoclassical view. However, the trouble is that traditional theory abstracts from risks and uncertainty whereas, in reality, the effect of uncertainty is to cause economies in capital investment by reducing the time during which funds are recouped from profits.

D.P.: In other words, you would not agree with recommendations such as the ones put forward by Professor Seers[39] to my country's government in the employment report in which he concludes that it is necessary to change the relative prices of the factors of production in order to foster employment.

Professor Kaldor: I think that there is no empirical support for that link: you can reduce the rate of interest (as some countries have done) and no significant employment generation follows.

D.P.: Another criticism that one could advance against your model of income distribution is that if one introduces another income group, let us say the rentiers (people who derive a rent from owning a factor of production), the conclusions you derive in connection with the relation between the rate of profit and the rate of growth, no longer hold.[40]

---

38. $\dfrac{I}{Y} = \dfrac{dk \times dY}{dY\, dT} \quad \dfrac{I}{Y} = kG = S$

    (G=growth rate, I=investment, k = marginal capital-product relation, K = capital, Y = total income, S = global savings rate)

39. D. Seers et al, *Hacia el pleno empleo*, Bogotá, 1970.

40. $Y = W+P$
    $S = Sw + Sp$
    $I = SpP + SwW$

    (G = growth rate, k = marginal capital-product relation, K = capital, Y = total income, S = global savings rate, I = investment, W = Wages, P = Profits, S = Savings, Sw = worker's savings, Sp = Capitalist savings.)

    It can be shown that $W/Y = Sp/Sp-Sw - I/Sp-Sw - I/Y$. In order to analyze Kaldor's theory of distribution, see N. Kaldor "Alternative Theories of Distribution," *Review of Economic Studies*. 1955.

Professor Kaldor: I agree that I do not explain how wages are distributed among workers of different skills, nor do I explain how profits are divided between rentiers and entrepreneurs. I do not think anybody has a good explanation of how distribution operates at this level. One can find many examples of historical differences in relative earnings, which have nothing to do with marginal productivities. Tradition establishes differentials that become socially acceptable. My theory only explains aggregate distribution and, in that sense, I accept your criticism.

D.P.: Another striking aspect of your model is that, if either capitalists or laborers succeed in understanding your theories, they could attempt to appropriate the whole income if they manage to choose the right savings ratio. Labor could appropriate all the social income by setting its savings ratio equal to the investment-income ratio chosen by the capitalists.[41]

Professor Kaldor: If workers decide to do that, they would starve, since their average propensity to consume is high.

D.P.: I am aware of that, but the important point to stress is that, if the distribution of income is governed by functional relationships, different income groups would alter their behavior as soon as they understood the operation of economic forces. Consequently, one would have to develop a sort of learning-by-doing process to consider this type of dynamic effect.

Professor Kaldor: That is equally true of other contexts. Buyers can understand that if they coordinate their actions they can exert monopsonic power. In that sense, what you point out is right: collusion brings benefits to the members of cartels.

Let me say that the first concrete result of my attempt to escape from the rigid framework of traditional theory was this macroeconomic theory of the share of profits in the value of output, which is different from the classical and neoclassical theories. It shows that profits are generated by entrepreneurial expenditures on investment.

D.P.: To what extent is this the Keynesian mechanism of aggregate income distribution that one encounters in the *Treatise on Money*?

---

41. $I = S_p P + S_w W$; If $S_w = I/Y$ then it can be proved that $P = O$.

Professor Kaldor: Although I was consciously influenced by Keynes's famous footnote on the "widow's curse" (*Treatise*), I am now aware that the Keynes's wartime pamphlet, "How to pay for the War," was the important influence.

D.P.: Now, let me say, that in reference to your technical progress function it appears to me that you have constructed a deterministic function of the flow of innovations which is against the logic of scientific discovery.

Professor Kaldor: I do not think it is deterministic. It is simply an assumption that has to do with the fact that new ideas accrue at a certain rate. This has been observed in an important number of cases and I consider it to be a reasonable assumption since the function has an important degree of stability.

D.P.: Some people have questioned the validity of your model since the assumptions required to produce a stable solution to the equations appear to be restrictive.

Professor Kaldor: I agree that some of the assumptions were restrictive, but the precise implications of the assumptions required for stability were only cleared up by Professor Champernowne in recent years.[42]

D.P.: In recent years we have seen several efforts at contrasting Keynes's and Marx's view of how the capitalist system works (J. Robinson, Dobb, Sweezy). I was wondering if you could point out what you consider to be the main differences between your approach (based on Keynesian postulates) and the traditional Marxist explanation.

Professor Kaldor: In 1956 I was given the opportunity of delivering a lecture at the University of Beijing. I took advantage of that occasion to pinpoint the main differences between Keynesian and Marxian economics insofar that the evolution of the capitalist system is concerned.

First of all, it is true that unemployment, cyclical fluctuation and concentration of property tend to appear in a free enterprise system. But these traits are not laws of the operation of the system as the Marxists

---

42. D.G. Champernowne, "The Stability of Kaldor's 1957 Model," *Review of Economic Study*, January 1971.

assume. After Keynes, we know that with adequate government controls and wise intervention we can counteract those tendencies.

It could be said that Marxist analysis is particularly applicable in the initial phase of capitalism, whereas Keynesian economics throws much more light on the operation of subsequent phases.

D.P.: After your 1957 growth model you worked on a "new" model of economic growth in collaboration with Mirrlees. What do you consider to be the main advancement of this effort in comparison with your earlier models?

Professor Kaldor: The main advancement of the new model was that it made explicit what was implicit with earlier models, that is to say, that technical progress is infused into the economic system through investment and it consequently becomes embodied in the construction of machinery. It captures, in this way, the phenomenon of technological obsolescence by assuming that once technology has been embodied, the production flowing from that equipment remains constant over time.

D.P.: Your models on growth and distribution give the impression that you had been using the method of deductive reasoning from macroeconomic axioms, without attempting to use empirical tendencies that have been detected.

Professor Kaldor: That comment is right. I gradually became aware that a more pragmatic approach could be more fruitful, and when I was working in the Treasury in the mid sixties, I came across a surprisingly close correlation between the rate of growth of manufacturing and the rate of growth of GDP. This association suggested that the rate of economic growth of a country will depend on how much faster its manufacturing output grows than the rest of the economy. This was an important insight to provide an explanation of why growth rates differed.

D.P.: I suppose you are referring to your inaugural lecture when you were appointed Professor of Economics at this University. You used a version of Verdoorn's law[43] to explain the poor performance of

---

43. In 1949 J. Verdoorn found evidence to postulate a relation between the productivity rate of growth and the production growth rate. See P.J. Verdoorn, "Fattori che regolano lo suiluppo della produttivita del lavoro." *L' Industria*, 1949.

the British economy in comparison with other countries. Following the publication of your lecture, several attempts were made to examine the theoretical and empirical foundations of your findings.[44] Rowthorn,[45] for instance, argues that there is no empirical evidence that your law has operated during the post-war period in the British manufacturing sector.

Professor Kaldor: Some people like Rowthorn thought that the main point I had put forward in my inaugural lecture was that the slow growth of the British economy was due to a shortage of labor. This was not the main message and, as I have acknowledged,[46] this particular hypothesis turned out to be a mistaken one. However, this did not invalidate my findings regarding the key role that the manufacturing industry plays in determining the growth rate.

D.P.: What do you consider to be the relative importance of supply and demand constraints in the determination of the growth potential of a mature economy such as Britain?

Professor Kaldor: It is the growth of demand for manufactures and not the supply constraints that determines how quickly the total output will grow. The recognition of the key role of the manufacturing industry made me aware that my single sector growth models we were discussing had fundamental shortcomings. The Keynesian features of the economy only apply to the industrial sector of the economy. The primary sector is governed by other forces and its growth rate depends on the progress of land-saving innovations. Moreover, increasing returns to scale are much more important in the manufacturing sector of the economy. Since industry is subject to what Myrdal calls the principle of circular and cumulative causation, free trade tends to enlarge differences in comparative costs and not to reduce them as neoclassicals postulate.

---

44. See for instance S. Gomulka, *Incentive Activity, Diffusion and the Stages of Economic Growth*, 1971.
45. R. Rowthorn, "What Remains of Kaldor's Law?", *Economic Journal*, March 1975
46. N. Kaldor, "Economic Growth and the Verdoorn Law: A Comment on Mr. Rowthorn's Article," *Economic Journal*, December 1975.

D.P.: I suppose you are referring to the theoretical alternative you proposed in your lecture at the Universidad de Barcelona.[47] After reading your paper I was left somewhat confused on how it is that the terms of trade between agriculture and industry are established. You state that the forces that govern industrial and agricultural prices are independent, but of course, you are neglecting the impact of tariff structures, which usually discriminate against agriculture as reflected in the Latin American import substitution strategies.

Professor Kaldor: Well, I have been explaining my ideas for the last ten years but only recently have I considered them sufficiently mature to merit publication. In addition to the conference you mention, I delivered an address as President of the Royal Economic Society,[48] which is complementary to my conferences at Barcelona and Harvard.

In that lecture I applied the analytical framework of my two-sector model to the problems of the world economy. I asserted that stable economic progress requires that the growth of output in the primary and secondary sectors should be at a required relation with each other. However, there is no guarantee that the growth rate of primary production proceeds at the rate required by the growth of production and incomes in the other sectors of the economy.

With reference to the terms of trade, let me say that the market price to producers and consumers involved in the primary sector is given in a competitive framework such as the one described by A. Smith. In industry, however, prices are not market clearing but they are fixed in an administrative way. This asymmetry implies that the burden of any unbalance between the growth of primary production and the growth of manufacturing industry significantly affects the former sector. On the other hand, a shift in the terms of trade in favor of primary producers cannot be permanent because the industrial sector can counteract the rise in commodity prices through a cost-induced inflation of manufactured prices.

Insofar as import substitution strategies are concerned, I would say that in order to achieve a sustained growth in the manufacturing sector, it is necessary first to develop a highly efficient primary sector. The growth of primary production establishes the limits to

---

47. N. Kaldor, "Teoría del Equilibrio y Teoría del Crecimiento," University of Barcelona, Spain, 1973.
48. N. Kaldor, "Inflation and Recession in the World Economy," *Economic Journal*, December 1976.

growth and governs the rate of growth of the system. Consequently, it is vital to organize a strong and stable primary sector in any economy, aiming at a high income per capita.

D.P.: I don't agree with you when you state that commodity prices are set in the manner described by A. Smith. Many important commodities (such as oil and copper) are traded in oligopolistic contexts and the explanatory power of most of the econometric models, that are based on the assumption of perfect competition, leaves much to be desired.

Professor Kaldor: Well, it is true I did not take into account that aspect of market structure. However, I think one can say that commodity prices are determined in the market, even if it is an oligopolistic market, whereas, industrial prices are cost determined. They are reached by applying mark-ups on costs on accounts of overheads and profits.

D.P.: In your Presidential Address to the Royal Economic Society you reach the conclusion that the most important challenge facing the world economy is the need to strengthen the adjustment mechanism between the growth of supply and demand for primary products. You then insist on your idea of introducing greater stability into the world economy by means of the international buffer stocks. I think your idea is clear but it seems to me you are overlooking the fact that primary commodities differ between themselves in very important ways. Consequently one needs to be very careful in the selection of a stabilization device. The government's choice should be guided by comparing the present value of the net excess social benefit resulting from alternative types of devices. There are an important number of such control devices: multilateral contracts, compensatory finance, buffer funds, export quotas, etc.; and each one has greater or lesser advantages depending on the commodity in question. In short, I do not consider that the generalization you have proposed is valid.

Professor Kaldor: Export-quota agreements could be the alternative. However, as I stated in a paper written some years ago,[49] they

---

49. N. Kaldor, "Stabilizing the Terms of Trade of Underdeveloped Countries," in *Essays on Economic Policy*. Vol. II.

are difficult to negotiate and they are likely to break down because of various reasons: Failure to secure participation of all producing countries, failure to regulate the domestic production of the exporting countries and the impossibility of freezing the pattern of world production and trade for more than a limited period. For these reasons I prefer to propose the use of buffer stocks as I explained in the paper I wrote with Hart and Tinbergen.[50]

D.P.: Every control device faces particular problems. Buffer stocks, for instance, have to deal with the problem of finance, which many times is beyond the possibilities of producers, and lacks the support of consumers.

Professor Kaldor: That is true and that is why I have proposed to link the finance of these stocks directly to the issue of an international currency, such as the SDRs.

D.P.: Another assertion of your Presidential Address that drew my attention was your statement implying that it would be wrong to suppose that the great acceleration of inflation of the last few years was the inevitable consequence of the long creeping inflation that preceded it.

In contrast to your position, Brunner and Meltzer[51] undertook an empirical investigation using data for five of the most important developed countries and conclude that the sustained and accelerating inflation emerging since the sixties evidently results from gradual shifts in budgetary and monetary policies of western countries.

Professor Kaldor: Brunner and Meltzer are curiously blind to the distinctions between the primary and secondary sectors of the economy. It seems to me futile to look for a single cause of the important acceleration of inflation in recent years, such as the increase in the money supply in all countries.

D.P.: Turning to another topic, it would be interesting to discuss some of the issues you presented at the Conference on Fiscal Policy for Economic Growth in Latin America which was held in Santiago

---
50. N. Kaldor, A. Hart and J.Tinbergen, "The Case for an International Commodity Reserve Currency," UNCTAD, 1964.
51. Brunner and Meltzer, A.E.R. February 1977.

in 1962.[52] Tax reforms continue to be a very controversial issue in Latin America. As a matter of fact, my government introduced a new scheme of taxation based to a certain extent on the recommendations of Professor Musgrave.[53] The main changes could be summarized as follows: (a) In general terms, the tax system was conceived as an instrument for income distribution and not so much as providing incentives for growth; (b) the sales tax was reformed to re-direct aggregate demand towards mass-produced goods; (c) personal and inheritance taxes were made more progressive; (d) a presumptive tax was introduced in the agricultural sector.

Given your experience with various tax reforms (India, Mexico, etc.) what is your reaction to this type of change in fiscal policy?

Professor Kaldor: The problem of accelerated economic development, in my view, is closely linked to the efficient provision of a large set of public goods commonly known as infrastructure (education, health, transport, etc.). I think a limitation of resources and not lack of adequate incentives ultimately limit the rate of economic growth. Now, it is clear to me that the taxation potential of a poor country is generally lower than that of a rich country and thus, over ambitious goals in public finance, should be adjusted to reality. In addition to the domestic effort, foreign aid should complement it but of course not substitute it.

D.P.: Would you agree with Musgrave[54] that the question of the proper size of the public sector is, to a significant degree, a technical rather than an ideological issue? Musgrave asserts that government regulation must secure the conditions of free entry and must face the problem derived from the existence of externalities that lead to market failure.

Professor Kaldor: I don't think there is an "optimal" size of the public sector. Government intervention is needed when the administration can deal better with the problem of uncertainty, as in the case of setting up projects that involve large investments such as steel plants.

---

52. N. Kaldor, "The Role of Taxation in Economic Development." Santiago, December 1962.
53. R. Musgrave et al., *Bases para una reforma tributaria en Colombia*, Bogotá, 1969.
54. R. Musgrave, *The Theory of Public Finance*, Tokyo, 1959.

D.P.: I think that the trouble with many tax reforms is that they overlook the fact that inefficient bureaucratic systems can appropriate the additional revenue generated, without any significant increase in the flow of public goods.

Professor Kaldor: The efficacy of a tax system is certainly not just a matter of well-designed tax laws but, to an important degree, it depends upon the efficiency and honesty of the administration. This is the most important requirement for an effective tax reform.

D.P.: Some people have accused you of delaying economic development in the countries where you have recommended tax reforms, because of the high degree of political instability introduced into the system.

Professor Kaldor: My role as a tax specialist has earned me a lot of unpopularity. In India and Ceylon, the governments I advised had to face very strong opposition. In Mexico and Turkey, which were in urgent need of efficient and honest tax reforms, the proposals could not be put into practice on account of opposition of the ruling classes. I think my advice was not wrong, it was only a matter of underestimating the political obstacles to make them effective.

D.P.: Following Musgrave[55] one could assert that fiscal policy has three major functions: the allocative, the distributive and the stabilization function. Which function do you think is the most important?

Professor Kaldor: I think that in less developed countries, progressive taxation is the only alternative to violent revolution. However, I have now become skeptical of the distributive function of tax policy. The ruling classes in the majority of developing countries are too powerful to allow an important reduction in their standard of living.

D.P.: You have recommended a personal expenditure tax as a supplement to an imperfectly functioning income tax, especially because of ineffective progression at high-income levels. What was your experience with this type of tax in India?

---

55. R. Musgrave, op.cit.

Professor Kaldor: The problem is that high taxes imply high bribes, and thus, the proposals I made were not effective.

D.P.: To end this interesting discussion, I would like to ask you the following question: After all the drawbacks and flaws you have attributed to mainstream economics, could one say that our discipline is passing through a very critical period with an uncertain future?

Professor Kaldor: It is true that at the moment, the status of economics appears to be chaotic and at the same time, many theoretical papers are becoming more abstract and irrelevant than ever. I think that the Keynesian voyage of intellectual discovery has brought solid results. We have now very important insights on how to manage a free enterprise system and we are very close to the solution of the problem of simultaneous achievement of the goals connected with growth and stability.

Bibliography

Brunner and Meltzer, *A.E.R.*, February 1977.
D.G. Champernowne, "The Stability of Kaldor's 1957 Model," *Review of Economic Studies*, January 1971.
Lauchlin Currie, *La enseñanza de la economía*, Bogotá, 1962.
A. Coale, *The Growth and Structure of Human Populations*, Princeton, 1972.
R.M. Cyert and M.H. de Groot, "An Analysis of Cooperation and Learning in a Duopoly Context," *American Economic Journal*, December 1972.
E. Denison, *Why Growth Rates Differ*, Brookings Institution, 1967.
S. Gomulka, *Incentive Activity, Diffusion and the Stages of Economic Growth*, 1971.
F. Hahn, "An Inaugural Lecture," Cambridge, 1973.
N. Kaldor, "Mrs. Robinson's Economics of Imperfect Competition," *Economica*, August 1934.
——, "Increasing Returns and Technical Progress: A Comment on Professor Hick's article," *Oxford Economic Papers*, February 1961.
——, "The Role of Taxation in Economic Development," Santiago, December 1962.
——, A. Hart and J. Tinbergen, "The Case for An International Commodity Reserve Currency," UNCTAD, 1964.
——, "Stabilizing the Terms of Trade of Less developed Countries," *Essays on Economic Policy, vol. II.1964*
——, "The Irrelevance of Equilibrium Economics," *Economic Journal*, December 1972.
——, "Teoría del equilibrio y teoría del crecimiento," Conference at the University of Barcelona, 1973.
——, "What Is Wrong With Economic Theory," *Quarterly Journal of Economics*, August 1975.
——, "Economic Growth and the Verdoorn Law: A Comment on Mr. Rowthorn's Articles," *Economic Journal*, December 1975.
——, "Inflation and Recession in the World Economy," *Economic Journal*, December 1976.
L.V. Kantorovich, *Essays in Optimal Planning*, Oxford, 1977.
A. López Toro, "Problems in Stable Population Theory," Princeton, 1961; "Asymptotic Properties of a Human Age Distribution Under a Continuous Net Fertility Function," *Demography*, 1967.
R. Musgrave et al, *Bases para una reforma tributaria en Colombia*, Bogotá, 1969.
R. Musgrave, *The Theory of Public Finance*, Tokyo, 1959.
D. Pizano, "A Conversation with Professor Joan Robinson," in this book.
C.F. Pratten, *Economies of Scale in Manufacturing Industry*, Cambridge University Press, 1971.
R. Rowthorn, "What Remains of Kaldor's Law?" *Economic Journal*, March 1975.
D. Seers et al., *Hacia el pleno empleo*, Bogotá, OIT, 1970.

A Conversation with
Professor Leonid V. Kantorovich

Ever since I started studying economics in 1968, the topic of the viability of centrally planned economies began to interest me. Over the years I had the opportunity to read various books on the topic, and, sometime around 1974, I prepared a document for the government of Colombia on international trade and central planning. It was at that time that I first came into contact with the writings of the Soviet Professor, Leonid Kantorovich (1912–1986). This distinguished scholar received the Nobel Prize in 1975, and it seemed to me that such an expert, who had worked on central planning at the highest levels, could greatly enhance the scope of my project. I therefore proceeded to contact the Professor early in 1978. Shortly thereafter he replied, accepting the idea of developing a structured dialogue. After a fairly complicated process I was able to obtain a visa to go visit him. It was at the height of the Cold War, in October, 1979, when our meeting finally took place.

Leonid V. Kantorovich was born in St. Petersburg, (Leningrad) on the 19th of January, 1912. In 1926 he enrolled in the mathematics department at the University of Leningrad, where he developed theorems in the area of set and set projection theory. The results of his research were presented at the First Mathematics Congress held in the Soviet Union in 1930. In 1934 he was confirmed as a full-time Professor of Mathematics at the University of Leningrad. In 1936, along with V. Krylow, he published a book on the new method of variations. In the thirties he became, quite by accident, interested in the problems of an industrial economy. This interest led him to become the first person in the world to formulate the theory of linear programming. During the war he worked as a Professor at the School of Naval Engineering. In 1944 he worked at the Institute for Mathematical Studies at the URSS Academy of Science, developing basic principles for the construction of computers. During the fifties he was concerned with the application of mathematics and cybernetics to the field of economics. In 1939 he published a book called, *The Best Use of Economic Resources*, a work he considers one of his principle contributions to the discipline of economics. Later he became a member of the USSR Academy of

Science and was the Director of the Center for the Application of Mathematics to the Economy, in Novosibirsk, Siberia. In 1965 he was awarded the Lenin Prize and, in 1975, the Nobel Prize. At the time we sustained the following dialogue he was the Director of the Institute for Control of the Soviet Economy, based in Moscow. This is where our meeting took place in late 1979.

The Conversation

Diego Pizano: I would like to separate this discussion into two main and distinct parts. In the first place, it would be interesting if we could treat some problems derived from the theory of planning and the contributions you have made to it. After that, if you agree, we could devote some time to the analysis of some aspects related to the recent evolution of the Soviet Economy and its future prospects.

The first issue I would like to introduce is the one concerned with the planning debate that has taken place in the West since the thirties and which still arouses an important degree of controversy. Let me first briefly summarize some of the main positions that have emerged in the discussions.

It is interesting to make reference first to the works of Pareto[56] and Barone.[57] These thinkers reached the conclusion that the necessary and sufficient conditions for achieving an optimal allocation of resources, given a social welfare function, were the same for a socialist and a free market economy. This conclusion differs radically from the one reached by Von Mises[58] who argued that a rational economic system and a socialist economy were incompatible. He considered that without the existence of labor, financial and goods markets it was impossible to determine a coherent system of prices.

Other economists like Robbins[59] agree with Pareto and Barone In the sense it could be possible to design a rational economic system within a socialist state, but the problem would be that the

---

56. Pareto, *Manuel d'économie politique*, Paris, 1927.
57. Barone, E. "The Ministry of Production in The Collectivist State," in F. Hayek (ed.), *Collectivist Economic Planning*, Routledge and Paul, London, 1935.
58. Von Mises, L., "Economic calculation in the Socialist Commonwealth," reprinted in Hayek, F.A. (ed.), *Collectivist Economic Planning*, London, 1935.
59. Robbins, L.C., *The Great Depression*, London, Macmillan, 1934.

prices could not be determined *a priori*. One would have to solve a system of simultaneous equations with thousands or perhaps millions of variables and this task is beyond the capabilities of the most sophisticated and modern computers.

Oscar Lange, in a well-known essay,[60] argued that there is a solution to the problem: the use of the market. He claims that there is no contradiction between the use of market forces and orthodox Marxism. He suggests a process of trial and error or *tatonnement*, which reminds one of the Walrasian *auctioneer*. This proposal has been rigorously analyzed by Arrow and Hurwicz.[61]

Finally, it is important to make reference to the influential work of Professor Hayek. He has questioned in various writings[62] the possibilities of successful planning on the grounds that it is impossible to make rational calculations in a moneyless economy because it is not possible to concentrate all the available knowledge in only one head or computer. He argues that we are not, as human beings, intellectually equipped (even with the aid of computers) to improve the functioning of a free market economy by adopting planning techniques without very considerably impairing productivity. It would be very interesting for the Western audience to know how you have reacted to this discussion.

Professor Kantorovich: The issue you have introduced is considered to be of the greatest importance in the Soviet Union and has received a great deal of attention in journals and publications of other socialist countries. I cannot get into a detailed analysis of all the ideas you have presented and thus I prefer to state my own position.

The capitalist system of production has existed for more than two hundred years and some of its principles were developed even earlier. The planned economy is much younger, therefore it is not surprising if all its problems have not been theoretically studied and all the practical knowledge is not yet readily available for solving an optimal socialist system. That is why not all of the advantages of state ownership of the means of production

---

60. Lange, O., "On the Economic Theory of Socialism," *Review of Economic Studies*, vol. 3, 1936.
61. K.J. Arrow and L. Hurwicz, "Descentralization and Computation in Resource Allocation," in *Essays in Economics and Econometrics in honor of Harold Hotelling*, Chapel Hill, 1960.
62. Hayek, F.A. (ed.), *Collectivist Economic Planning*, London, 1935.

have been used to its fullest extent. This explains why we have to witness some drawbacks. Many people, in the Soviet Union, are aware that our economic system is not perfect and the task of improving the planning system is constantly pressed by our party and our government. One of the most recent events in this field is a decision taken on July 12th 1979, concerning the improvement of planning and management problems. It is commonly believed that in order to solve the management problems and improve the methodology of planning models of economic optimization need to be introduced.

These models have been developed in the USSR with the aid of computers. These methods have already found partial employment in the planning organization of our country and in the automatic management system that exists in some advanced branches of the soviet industry. I want to stress a related point. Mathematical modeling has helped in the task of specifying the quantitative laws that govern socialist economies. It has made substantial contributions to the solution of key problems such as the following: (i) The problem of fixing the main economic variables; (ii) The measurement of the effectiveness of capital investment; (iii) The evaluation of national resources; (iv) More effective use of basic principles such as the ones concerned with the material balance methodology.

The laws of optimal planning generate a system of economic values (prices, rents, interest), which can be worked out together with the general plan and can be used for decision-making, providing an optimal decision-making procedure from the point of view of the economy. It is, of course, obvious that it is difficult to apply the principles of optimal planning in a simple way; but the very fact that objective, effective prices and economic values exist is of the greatest importance. I have shown that it is possible to derive objectively determined prices, or shadow prices, as Koopmans calls them. This analysis is considered to be contrary to the conclusions of people like Hayek and Von Mises. They thought that, since a planned economy has no stock exchange and no markets, there could not be an effective pricing system. The optimal model shows that in a planned economy there is a real possibility of arriving at an even more efficient pricing system than the one provided by the market system. This is particularly true with regard to the long-run economic decisions. Experience has shown that the capitalist system has drawbacks, which lead to overproduction and deficits.

In short, it must be said that in the thirties when the planning debate was taking place, the criticisms of Mises and Hayek were hard to answer. Nowadays, however, the development of the techniques of optimal planning has invalidated their conclusions.

D.P.: After having read some of the essays you have written on the theory of optimal planning,[63] I had the impression you were, perhaps unconsciously, rediscovering some of the principles developed by Walras in the last century. How do you relate Walras's work to your own work?

Professor Kantorovich: There is some relation between my models and Walras's because he also employed mathematical models. However, Walras developed his system with equilibrium equations and these were connected with the market economy. His approach was quite different and the purpose of his research was also dissimilar.

It could be said that my work is closer to the research undertaken by Pareto since his analysis has a more general character; nevertheless, it must be stressed that the theory of optimal planning is based on valuation methods and in the utilization of linear programming.

D.P.: Many people who studied linear programming methods find it difficult to apply these techniques for the solution of industrial problems given the fact that economies of scale and non-convexities in production functions are frequent phenomena. Consequently, it is not possible to deal with non-linearities with linear programming methods. What is your solution to this problem?

Professor Kantorovich: As it was already stated, beside practical utility, even the simplest linear programming methodology was a breakthrough in the sense that it showed that the mathematical approach was very illuminating for comprehension and solution of economic problems.

The effectiveness of mathematical economic models was demonstrated and we can compare this situation to Lagrange's mechanical equations of movement. In that case, only some problems of mechanics were solved; more complex ones were tackled with other

---

63. Kantorovich, L., *Essays in Optimal Planning*, Blackwell, Oxford, 1977.

techniques. However, the use of simple methodologies paved the way for understanding some problems of that field that had not been solved and the same can be said of linear programming. It can be efficient in solving certain problems. I agree it is not adequate for tackling others. Consequently, it is necessary to use a wide scope of scientific means in order to solve economic problems. Large numbers of techniques are being developed and we have applied not only linear programming but also discrete methods, planning by objectives, etc.

Another point that needs to be emphasized is that linear programming is better adapted to the conditions of a planned economy than to the characteristics of a capitalist system. It is a method that has been employed to solve problems regarding the rational distribution of products (pipes and rolling mills, for example); this is feasible when there is a single supply institution. It does not have the same applicability in Western type economies although developing countries use the method.

D.P.: Now that you have mentioned the planning techniques of some developing countries, I would like to point out that the input-output methods have been used as the basis of various planning exercises, particularly in Latin America (Colombia and Chile, for example). These exercises have not been very successful because it is very difficult to predict certain external conditions which these countries significantly depend on: foreign exchange and technology, for instance. On the other hand, the assumption of fixed technical coefficients is not very close to the real world and imposes real limits to the validity of short and long-term projections. What is the experience of the Soviet Union in applying these types of tools?

Professor Kantorovich: I have not used input-output models directly, but I am certainly familiar with them. Let me tell you that the aggregation techniques of these models lead to quite substantial drawbacks because the technical coefficients in relation to growth are very different from the average. The greatest difficulties are clearly encountered with dynamic calculations. In some cases, they result in absurd conclusions from the point of view of economics, and they have to be altered in an artificial way.

On the other hand, we have good experience at the Institute of Economics (Siberia) in resolving long-run economic problems. It has been demonstrated in my work and in papers written in collaboration with Dr. Makarow, a corresponding member of the Academy of Sciences, that it is feasible to apply dynamic linear programming methods. Professor Augustinovich of the Hungarian State Planning Office has also developed dynamic models based on the theory of stochastic programming. I witnessed how she worked with the computer and, in only one hour, she generated many different variants. Her work shows that it is possible to simulate changes in external conditions. I believe this approach would be suitable for the type of uncertainty problems you have mentioned with reference to developing countries.

D.P.: I find what you say about stochastic programming quite interesting. I must say, it reminds me of the scenarios method used by Professor Leontieff in his study of the future of the world economy.[64] However, even a mathematically minded economist like Leontieff thinks that the quantitative techniques are not sufficient for understanding the evolution and the prospects of any economy. Therefore he considers qualitative analysis is absolutely necessary. Would you agree with him?

Professor Kantorovich: I agree, in general, with his position. But I would add that mathematical models also give qualitative results related to structure. Nevertheless, it is necessary to use them very carefully as they are not universal. Mathematical models are receiving greater attention by our government since people are now aware that the introduction of elements of optimization into long-term planning will increase the level of return on capital and will lead to an efficient allocation of resources. However, the new methods are not being sufficiently used by our planning agencies. It is obvious new methods face many obstacles to be fully implemented.

D.P.: I have heard from some people that your proposals have been criticized in the Soviet Union on the grounds they could endanger the high rates of economic growth achieved with the traditional planning procedures. Is there any justification for this point of view?

Professor Kantorovich: That view is totally unfounded. Some people thought that because shadow prices expressed scarcity

---

64. Leontieff, W., *The Future of the World Economy*, Oxford, 1978.

constraints, the rate of growth would not be maintained. The truth is that these objectively determined prices will lead to an efficient path for economic growth.

D.P.: You are universally recognized as the founder of linear programming theory. As we all know, this theory was originally formulated in static terms and it was applied to microeconomic problems. How was it possible to extend the results of a micro-static framework to a macro-dynamic context?

Professor Kantarovich: In one of my first books, The *Best Use of Economic Resources*, I extended the results of linear programming from the level of the firm to a short-run model of the national economy. Later on, I developed a dynamic model[65] in which all shadow prices are dated and comparability between costs and benefits is assured by discounting future variables to their present values. I have designed models intended for optimization over time of which the short run model is just a one period cross-section. It has been a difficult task but it is feasible.

D.P.: How do you deal with the fact that economics is not an exact science and, therefore, it is next to impossible to put forward accurate predictions in the long run?

Professor Kantorovich: My plans are only partly deterministic. By necessity they have to have a probabilistic component, particularly in such areas as foreign trade and mineral exploration.

D.P.: Some people in the West associate your optimal planning methods with market socialism. To what extent is this correct?

Professor Kantorovich: The view is incorrect. Planning a complex economy requires the combination of a central plan with autonomous action by decentralized units. However, the decisive role corresponds to the national plan. Consequently, market forces are used only as a complementary mechanism to the optimal planning methodology.

---

65. Kantorovich, L., *A Dynamic Model of Optimum Planning*, Moscow, Nauka Publishers, 1964.

D.P.: I think we have already devoted enough time to the fascinating debate of some points related to the theory of planning. If you agree, we could turn now our attention to a brief analysis of some aspects concerned with the recent evolution of the soviet economy.

The first area I have selected is the energy balance of the USSR. The Soviet Union is the only big industrial nation that produces more energy than it consumes. It is still the world's largest producer of oil. Nevertheless, according to various experts in the West, people at the Russian Research Center at Harvard, for instance, the share of oil and natural gas in the energy equation of the USSR is declining. They also assert that, since one third of the national capital investment in the economy is already allocated to the energy sector, it is very difficult to intensify exploration activities. Do you think the Soviet Union is facing or will face an energy crisis in the near future (1980–83)?

Professor Kantorovich: To answer that complex question one would have to be a very knowledgeable geologist. All I can say is that the Soviet Union, as a whole, has a considerable number of different sources of energy (coal, natural gas, oil, hydroelectric power) and they are, to a great extent, interchangeable. Road transport could be replaced by electric or diesel trains. The employment of electrically propelled road vehicles is also a possibility. I am sure my country will not become a great oil importer. On the question of whether it will continue to be an important oil exporter, I am not qualified to answer.

D.P.: In Western countries such as Germany, there has been a considerable degree of controversy around the question of increasing the role of nuclear energy. Many people now believe that the costs of developing nuclear energy could exceed the benefits. What is the position of soviet experts on this matter?

Professor Kantorovich: I am not a nuclear expert, but it is my impression that the dangers associated with the development of nuclear energy have been exaggerated. I believe that the share of nuclear energy in the soviet energy sector will gradually increase over the next years.

D.P.: Another big issue that is actively being discussed in Western circles is the current state of soviet agriculture. Experts have pointed out that the level of grain output is not satisfactory. The protein content of feed grain is poor; adverse climate, lack of infrastructure, shortage of electricity, falling labor, and capital productivity all contribute to a situation of increasing food imports from the rest of the world. Do you think these rather pessimistic prospects about the agricultural sector of your country correspond to a real situation?

Professor Kantorovich: All these problems you have mentioned have been widely covered in our newspapers and scientific journals. It is common knowledge that the soviet agricultural sector has many unexploited possibilities. Advanced farms get twice as much output per unit of land than average and below average farms. A clear problem of efficiency of resource use exists here. Optimal planning models should be more widely used in agricultural programming to ensure that the factors of production are well allocated and managed.

D.P.: The demographic issue is another major area of concern. According to Dr. Boyarsky, Director of the Scientific Research Institute of the Central Statistical Administration of the USSR, the main demographic problems of the Soviet Union are: (a) A growing imbalance between the growth rates in the population of the various ethnic groups; (b) The general rise in mortality rates; (c) Reduction in the life expectancy of males; (d) A reduction in the rate of growth of the labor force.

Do you think these complex situations will impose constraints on the future growth prospects of the Soviet Union?

Professor Kantorovich: I consider that the growth of mortality and the reduction of life expectancies may be due to insignificant yearly variations. Life expectancy had grown in post-war years and is still at a very high level; consequently small variations should not be stressed. The low growth rate of the labor force in some age groups is due to a diminishing rate of migration from the countryside to the main cities. This fact causes some difficulties, of course, but we are working out some methods to increase the supply of labor such as employing pensioners. Another measure could be to promote a more rational distribution of labor and to employ more women. On the other hand, the productivity of labor has to increase. I think that with these types of methods we shall be in a position to cope with the problems you have mentioned.

D.P.: With reference to the causes of the changes in the Soviet economy's growth rate, alternative theories have emerged. It seems clear that the economy is not growing as fast as it once did in previous decades. Could this be a result of a foreign exchange gap, a savings gap and a consequence of the energetic, agricultural and demographic constraints we were discussing?

Professor Kantorovich: It is true that the Soviet economy's growth rate has decreased. The main causes of this situation could be summarized as follows: In the first place, the size of the economy is much greater and this fact, in itself, leads to a decrease in the growth rate. Second, we now have shortages of some natural resources, particularly in the western regions. Third, the increased scale of production and the technical difficulties associated with growth need improved management. Adjustments are being carried out at present but will not give results very quickly. Fourth, a lot of funds have been channeled to long-range projects such as hydroelectric power stations, railways, etc., which, of course, require time to yield results. Finally, the calculation of the rate of growth in price terms is difficult and not precise. Other methods lead to higher rates.

D.P.: Ever since East–West trade began to expand seriously in the sixties, the Soviet Union began to show balance of payments problems. Net soviet debt has increased to over twenty billion dollars from the West. According to a Hungarian economist, I. Vajda, these problems result from an inability to compete successfully in the international market of goods and services. This situation is a consequence of deficiencies in performance, lack of know-how, bad packaging and appearance and inadequate after-sale services. Others argue that the size of rewards for innovation are not big enough to overcome risk and inertia, and that domestic pricing is irrational. Which of these hypotheses, in your opinion, is closest to the truth?

Professor Kantorovich: It is true that factors like adverse climate and such have created balance of payments problems. I would say that many enterprises are good enough in terms of production targets, but not sufficiently well managed to successfully sell in international markets.

D.P.: One of the issues that is currently being discussed in international seminars and conferences is one related to the connection that exists—and should exist—between science, technology and production. Most informed people agree that in the case of the Soviet Union, there is an important scientific community undertaking original research in many areas but functioning quite apart from the technical and managerial people. Consequently, it appears that important scientific discoveries do not lead in many cases to an increase in the technical level of production. Is this true?

Professor Kantorovich: It is true in some cases and the same can be said of many Western countries! The gap between science, technology and production should be closed or at least reduced in a significant way. Our government is aware of the problem and measures are being taken in order to deal with this important matter.

D.P.: One of the most difficult decisions developing countries must face is the decision of to what extent they should try to select, adapt and generate technologies instead of indiscriminately importing know-how. What light does the Soviet Union experience shed for developing countries with a growing industrial base such as Colombia and Mexico?

Professor Kantorovich: Scientific and technical progress is the most essential mechanism to increase the production growth rate in any economy. The level of science and the adoption and diffusion of new techniques determine a country's economic potential. It is very important to encourage, not only the natural sciences, but also the social sciences, including economics. The advances made in mathematical economics and cybernetics has made this discipline come closer to the problems of the real world than ever before.

I think that the Soviet Union has to become self-sufficient in science and technology. Smaller economies, including socialist and developing countries, must continue to import more general types of technology in a selective way and should try to increase the added value of their natural resources by adapting, and eventually generating, specific types of techniques.

D.P.: What do you consider to be the main unresolved problem in the theory of optimal planning?

Professor Kantorvich: Many of the ideas included in the theory of optimal planning, which have been mentioned in this discussion, have not yet been fully implemented. The main task, now, is to adapt the theoretical framework for effective use at the industrial level and the economic planning process.

There are many unresolved problems: Ecological issues, and the modeling of global interdependence among others. There are more problems to be solved than are solved.

D.P.: What do you consider to be the most important economic theories at the world level?

Professor Kantorovich.: I think that the works of Keynes and his school, the works of Leontieff and Von Neumann, and the works of soviet economists in the sphere of the theory of planning and its implementation, are the most important contributions.

D.P.: What do you regard as your most important personal contribution?

Professor Kantorovich: The development of the linear programming theory, forty years ago, and my book, *The Best Use of Economic Resources,* published twenty years ago, which provided the basis for the theory of optimal planning.

Bibliography

K.J. Arrow and L. Hurwicz, "Decentralization and Computation in Resource Allocation," in *Essays in Economics and Econometrics, In Honor of Harold Hotelling*, Chapel Hill, 1960.

Barone, E. "The Ministry of Production in the Collectivist State," in F. Hayek (ed.) *Collectivist Economic Planning*, Routledge and Paul, London, 1935.

Hayek, F.A. (ed.), *Collectivist Economic Planning*, London, 1935.

——, *Individualism and Economic Order*, London, 1976.

Kantorovich, L., *A Dynamic Model of Optimum Planning*, Moscow, Nauka Publishers, 1964.

——, *Essays in Optimal Planning*, Blackwell, Oxford, 1977.

——, Nobel Prize Lecture, Stockholm, 1975.

——, *The Best Use of Economic Resources*, Moscow, 1958.

Koopmans, I.J., "A Note about Kantorovich's Paper, Mathematical Methods of Organizing and Planning Production," *Management Science*, 1960.

Lange, O., "On the Economic Theory of Socialism," *Review of Economic Studies*, Vol. 3, 1936.

Leontieff, W., *The Future of the World Economy*, Oxford, 1978.

Pareto, V., *Manuel d'economie politique*, Paris, 1927.

Pizano, D., "Comercio exterior y planificación central," unpublished paper, Bogotá, 1977.

Robbins, L.C., *The Great Depression*, London, Macmillan, 1934.

Von Mises, L., "Economic calculation in the Socialist Commonwealth," reprinted in Hayek (1935).

A Conversation with Professor Joan Robinson

When I arrived at Cambridge in August of 1972, to begin my postgraduate studies, I decided to contact Professor Joan Robinson. She was a controversial figure due to her confrontations with economists of the traditional school and because of her opinions on Chinese centralized planning. I thought it would be interesting to visit her: Keynes had considered her the most brilliant of his collaborators and she was also known to be interested in the problems of developing countries. She welcomed me kindly and referred to some of her experiences in countries such as China, India and Mexico. Afterwards I attended several of her conferences. Some years later I wrote to her to inform her of my project and told her that I believed it was important that the book include representatives of the Keynesian school. She accepted the proposal enthusiastically and received me in her office in late July 1977.

Joan Robinson (1903–1983) was Emeritus Professor at the University of Cambridge at the time this dialogue took place. Among her books are the following: *Economics of Imperfect Competition* (1931), *Essays in the Theory of Employment* (1937), *An Essay on Marxian Economics* (1942), *Collected Economic Papers*, *vol. I* (1951), *vol. II* (1960), *vol. III* (1965), and *vol. IV* (1973), *The Accumulation of Capital* (1956), *Essays in the Theory of Economic Growth* (1962), *Economics: An Awkward Corner* (1966), and *Economic Philosophy* (1962). She is the only woman who has been a finalist for the Nobel Prize for Economics. She had academic exchanges with renowned economists such as Professors Joseph Schumpeter, Paul Samuelson and Milton Friedman. A list of her most distinguished students would include Amartya Sen, awarded the Nobel Prize for Economics; A.J. Kregel, Professor at Johns Hopkins University; and M. Singh, Prime Minister of India. On the occasion of her first centenary an interesting book was published on her life and work.[66]

---

66. Gibson, B.(ed.), *Joan Robinson's Economics, A Centennial Celebration*, Elgar, 2005.

The Conversation

Diego Pizano: In your 1949 article, "Mr. Harrod's Dynamics,"[67] you suggested that Keynesian dynamics could be applied to the problems of underdeveloped countries. This idea has been adopted by many planners to judge by the impact the Harrod-Domar models have in plans adopted by many countries in Latin America. Yet there is an increasing dissatisfaction with the results and achievements of economic planning.[68] As discussed with Professor Tinbergen,[69] this situation could be partially explained by governments lacking the degree of commitment required to really stick to their plans. In addition, Harrod and Domar formulations have their conceptual complications and drawbacks, which reduce their applicability. I think special problems arise when adopting the short-run model elaborated by Keynes, and even Harrod's contribution, to the long-run problems of developing countries. Nonetheless, national income analysis owes a great deal to Keynes and it is useful: It is evident that without this framework discussing economic development in an operationally significant way would be quite difficult.

To make my position clear from the outset, what I want to argue is that it is misleading to transplant Keynesian ideas including post-Keynesian development to developing countries without important qualifications and adjustments. One of the major lessons that Keynes can teach the developing world is his method of approaching economic problems (as I will argue later, his epistemological principles) and not the blind adoption of the functional relationships he specifies for the British Economy of the thirties. I am not denying that concepts like liquidity preference and the multiplier are extremely useful, but his ideas must be adapted. The extension of his model by Harrod should also be treated with caution and not applied without significant adjustments.

Professor Robinson: As I stated in my *Economic Philosophy*[70] in the post-war period, after the problem of deficient effective demand

---

67. J. Robinson, "Mr. Harrod's Dynamics," (review) *Economic Journal*, March 1949.
68. See for example, D. Seers (ed.), *The Crisis in Planning*, Edinburgh, 1972.
69. D. Pizano, "A Conversation with Professor Jan Tinbergen," in this book.
70. J. Robinson, *Economic Philosophy*, London, 1962.

was tackled with Keynesian tools, a fresh question came to the fore: Long-run development.

This change of emphasis, from the short-run to the long-run was brought about by the emergence of new nations, but also because of the internal evolution of economics as an academic discipline. The Keynesian theory of the short period was then firmly established and we all know that the main role here is played by the rate of investment. So it was natural to ask what could be the consequences, for the economic system, of the accumulation of capital that investment generates. In this context, both static neoclassical analysis, and Keynesian short run analysis of how given resources are employed, seems inadequate.

As I pointed out in my *Economic Heresies*,[71] the weakest point in neoclassical doctrine is that technical progress is considered an occasional shock that shifts the equilibrium position of the system. Harrod begins to treat the matter more realistically since he assumes that technical progress can be considered a built-in propensity of the economic system.

The great merit of Harrod's model is that it is not an equilibrium scheme. It is a projection into the long-run of some of the concepts of the *General Theory*. The rate of accumulation is a function of the decisions taken by profit-seeking enterprises and there is no guarantee that the rate of investment will be at the desired level in a market economy. Unfortunately, neoclassicals like Swan[72] seized upon Harrod's model and tried to convert it into a pre-Keynesian one.

D.P.: I agree that the Harrod model was a significant breakthrough, but I would like to point out that his conceptual framework has a number of complications which limit its applicability in the context of less developed countries:

(i) As you have asserted in one of your essays, the case he contemplates (capital accumulation outrunning population growth) is not typical; one should assume quite the contrary in the elaboration of the natural rate. Of equal importance is the fact that the natural growth rate depends on technological improvements and he does not delve into the issue of the

---

71. J. Robinson, *Economic Heresies*, London, 1971.
72. T. Swan, "Growth Models of Golden Ages and Production Functions," in *Economic Development*, K. Berrill (ed,), London, MacMillan, 1964.

nature of the expected innovations. He arbitrarily envisages a constant labor-output ratio as well as a constant capital-output ratio, and these are not backed by the empirical evidence available for developing countries. I am not claiming it is at all easy to treat technical progress. On the contrary, it might be the crucial stumbling block.

(ii) Harrod conceives an economy in which the propensity to save tends to exceed the inducement to invest. This makes his model too explosive in the sense that it postulates a persistent tendency toward cyclical deflation and chronic stagnations. I think that what Hicks calls "coolants"[73] must be introduced, particularly autonomous investment which allows the possibility of incorporating a variety of different types of shocks.

(iii) The warranted rate of Harrod's model is certainly based on Keynes doctrine of effective demand. It cannot be understood except in the context of insufficient effective demand and what Keynes calls involuntary unemployment. But the empirical studies that are available in countries such as Colombia suggest that unemployment is not of the Keynesian type. If there is structural unemployment, it is evident that the Harrod formulation would not offer us a framework for understanding the real causes of unemployment.

Professor Robinson: First of all, as I have stated elsewhere, Keynes's theory was framed entirely in the context of an advanced industrial economy with highly developed financial institutions. The problem of unemployment that concerned Keynes was accompanied by under-utilization of capacity already in existence. The unemployment of underdeveloped economies arises because productive capacity and effective demand have never been at an appropriate level. However, as I have pointed out in some of my writings, Keynesian economics can shed light on the solution of some problems of economic policy in less developed countries, although in a negative way. Let's take, for example, the problem of inflation. The *General Theory* shows, in a very convincing manner, that inflation is a *real* and not a *monetary* phenomenon. There is still a widespread belief that inflation is a monetary problem that can be controlled by means of manipulating the supply of currency. But the fact is that many

---

73. See D. Pizano, "A Conversation with Professor John Hicks," in this book.

professional economists and influential politicians have not yet understood one of the essential propositions of the *General Theory*: the level of money wage rates governs the level of prices. It is not clear at all that the so-called Cambridge equation[74] TT=kY/M, or the Fisher equation[75] (MV=PT) really explain reality. They are only simple tautologies. Let me illustrate this by presenting the Quantity Equation for hairpins, which Lord Kahn set out in the thirties as a protest against this wrong view of this theory of money.[76] Let's define the following variables P=proportion of women with long hair, T=total number of women; 1/V daily loss of hairpins by each woman with long hair, and M=the daily output of hairpins. Then, M=PT/V and that implies that MV=PT.

Now, assume that the Pope wishes to increase the proportion of longhaired women in the population on the grounds that short hair is not compatible with good morals, and so he asks an economic advisor what would be the best thing to do. The economist explains to the Pope the Quantity Equation for hairpins and gives him the magic formula: you have to increase M, the daily output of hairpins and the number of longhaired women will increase! But if the Pope is not convinced, the economist could recommend persuading the longhaired women to lose less hairpins and V would increase. The effect would be the same as if M had increased. When the experts on money realized their simple equations did not have causal significance, they were left with an uneasy feeling. The simple truisms could explain anything that had happened, but they did not have the basis for predicting what would happen next.

In the context of less developed nations, the concept of effective demand helps us understand the causes of inflation. If there is an increase in effective demand (let us say as a consequence of a favorable evolution of the terms of trade), prices will normally rise because the elasticity of supply of goods is usually low. The higher cost of living that results from this process will set up a pressure to raise wage rates. Money incomes will be increased as a consequence and the vicious spiral of inflation sets into the operation of the system.

---

74. TT = buying power of money; Y = real national income; k = proportion of national income kept as money; M = quantity of money.
75. M = monetary offer; V = velocity of money; P = price level; T = national income.
76. J. Robinson, "The Theory of Money and the Analysis of Output," *R.E.S.*, October 1933.

There are other interesting contributions Keynesian economics can make to the understanding of the problem of development (foreign aid, for example). But let me make a few remarks about Harrod's contribution. I summarized a long period of discussion around Harrod's work in a paper I published in the *Economic Journal* a few years ago.[77] I think that one of the main points of Harrod's contribution is very important: Actual economies cannot be expected to grow at a steady and desirable rate without control and direction. But I do agree when you say the framework has got drawbacks when used as a model for development planning. I would say that Kalecki's contributions could be more relevant.

D.P.: In addition to your remarks, I would say that there are at least two important concepts developed by Keynes which could be adapted in the case of a country such as Colombia: (a) the Multiplier theory, in particular the foreign trade multiplier and (b) The concept of liquidity preference which is highly relevant not only for understanding stock market performance and monetary problems, but is a great help in understanding the behavior of commodity prices, in particular of futures markets.

I understand Kalecki did work with many ideas quite close to the *General Theory*. Yet I do not recall that he takes into account the multiplier doctrine and the liquidity preference approach. Would you agree?

Professor Robinson: First of all I must say that M. Kalecki discovered the basic elements of the theory of saving, investing and employment before Keynes had fully worked out his *General Theory*. The question of dates is not important apart from the fact it shows that simultaneity in the discovery of important principles is possible in economics. What is important is that in several respects Kalecki's theory is clearer and stronger than Keynes's.

Kalecki's system was based on the Marxian framework of reproduction. He was able to extract from Marx the determination of effective demand, a task at which nobody had succeeded before him. Now I agree with you, he does not work with the multiplier in the sense that he lacks an explicit exposition but he works with a similar idea. He provides an explanation (different from Keynes)

---

77. J. Robinson, "Harrod after Twenty-One Years," *Economic Journal*, September 1970.

of the process by which an increase in investment induces an increase in savings. Instead of relying on the consumption function (Keynes), Kalecki shows that an increase in investment brings about increased savings by raising profits relatively to wages. Now, instead of confusing the stage with the *ex-ante, ex-post* controversy Kalecki simply assumes that a rise in the rate of investment will increase the flow of wages, which will be spent, and if the parallel rise in profits, causes an increase in spending out of dividends, profits will rise by so much the more. Consequently, as I explain in a recent paper,[78] Kalecki shows that there is an increase in retained profits equal to the increased outlay on investment.

On the other hand, one could accept he lacks the explicit formulation of the multiplier theory, but he elaborated a theory of the trade cycle on which Keynes was very weak. His analysis is based on the distinction between investment decisions and actual investment. He shows how a higher level of investment means a higher level of profits. Therefore, a higher expected rate of profit, therefore enlarged investment and so the self-winding process of boom is under way. But this process cannot go on indefinitely because no individual enterprise can command an indefinitely large amount of finance at the given rate of interest.

In relation to the monetary aspect of the theory I think Kalecki's version was much more elaborate than Keynes's. His distinction between actual investment and investment plans allows him to sidetrack many of the confusions and muddles Keynes did not manage to avoid. Keynes's schedule of the marginal efficiency of capital confuses the future expectations of profits of individual firms with the profits that will be realized for the industry taken globally. Kalecki's approach is much clearer: Conditions today influence investment decisions in the process of being taken and they will affect the conditions that prevail in the future when they are being carried out.

D.P.: What was Keynes's reaction to the propositions developed by Kalecki which you have presented?

Professor Robinson: Well, when Kalecki visited Cambridge in 1936, Keynes was not much impressed with him and his ideas. Keynes

---

78. J. Robinson, "Michael Kalecki on the Economics of Capitalism," *Oxford Bulletin of Economics and Statistics*, February 1977.

was thinking of rewriting the *General Theory* in a completely different way and he did not have the patience to hear about other people's theories at the time.

D.P.: In what main respects was Keynes thinking in changing his *General Theory*?

Professor Robinson: Well, he was unhappy with his theory of interest and with the clarity of some of his concepts. He was disappointed because very few people understood what the *General Theory* was really about.

D.P.: I would like to come back to Keynes in a moment, but, since we are talking about the relevance of growth models for the developing countries, I want to make a very brief remark on your *Accumulation of Capital*.[79]

I think that it could be argued that the essential features of your model are not very different from the theoretical structures of Harrod and Domar. What strikes me is that you assume that capital-accumulation depends on the profit-wage relation as well as on labor productivity, whereas Harrod and Domar assume it depends on the savings ratio and the productivity of capital. Would this difference imply that Harrod and Domar are closer than you in this respect to Keynes?

On the other hand, with reference to the problem of instability, do you consider your model as extremely unstable? I say this because you tend to suggest that the equilibrating mechanisms are not very strong.

I think a very important question should be asked about the models I am talking about (Harrod, Hicks, and Robinson, etc.). Are these growth models really dynamic? As commented in a recent conversation I had with Professor Hicks,[80] it is not clear that growth theorists were fair with Keynes's view of an irrevocable past and an uncertain future. The steady state technique and the dating of variables only gives the impression of an economy set up in time. By making present behavior depend on past experience it gives the illusion of the Greek concept of the tri-dimensionality of time but it leaves no room for the unexpected. The trouble is that

---

79. J. Robinson, *The Accumulation of Capital*, London, 1956.
80. See "A Conversation with Professor John Hicks," in this book.

in the steady state any point in time is similar to any other, thus growth theorists have neglected time, the crucial variable in their analysis. I think this criticism can be applied to Harrod's model but it is my impression that it could apply to some parts of your growth models and golden ages.

Professor Robinson: I use the golden age as an intellectual experiment in growth theory and not as a hypothesis. The chief merit of this procedure is that it allows me to imagine a historical path (not necessarily an equilibrium path) in which the rate of accumulation (ex-ante), the physically possible rate and the boundary conditions happen to be compatible. It is interesting because it sheds light on various kinds of disharmony. As a matter of fact at the end of book II, I show why the conditions of the golden age are not likely to be fulfilled. The golden age only indicates a mythical state of affairs, not likely to be found in any actual economy. But it is necessary to describe these conditions to show how far capitalist economies are from the states of tranquility, lucidity and harmony. The rules of the capitalist game of production have been developed to make accumulation and technical progress possible in conditions of disequilibrium (uncertainty, imperfect knowledge, etc.). However, if a free market economy is subject to external shocks and internal contradictions, it is not likely to survive. The survival of capitalism, up to now, is evidence that a certain decree of coherence exists within its confusion.

Finally, what you tell me about Professor Hicks is very interesting. It seems as though he assimilates my ideas very slowly, and he places them very deep in his subconscious and then one begins to see that they start to emerge gradually in his written work, a fascinating psychological process indeed!

D.P.: Another aspect that reduces the potential applicability of growth models in our time is the lack of awareness regarding the relationships that exist between economics and biology. Keynes suggested in *Economic Possibilities for our Grandchildren*,[81] that the future rate of economic progress would depend on: (a) our power to control population, (b) our determination to avoid wars, (c) our willingness to entrust to science the direction of those matters

---

81. J.M. Keynes, *Essays in Persuasion*, Collected Works, London, MacMillan, 1971.

which are properly the concern of science, and (d) the rate of accumulation as fixed by the margin between our production and our consumption. On the basis of what he estimated to be the combined powers of technical progress and compound interest Keynes predicted a utopia where the economic problem would disappear and men could be highly spiritual and would act according to desirable moral principles. But I think he overlooked a major point which was stressed by his master, A. Marshall, and that was that he did not regard economics as a continuation of the biological process as the eminent physicist A. Lotka has suggested.[82] If the economic process consists of the transformation of energy as the entropy law dictates, it is evident that it is indispensable to include the rate of depletion of natural resources and the limits derived from the scarcity of raw materials in any model which attempts to explain reality.

Professor Robinson: I do agree with most of the things you said. Keynes was certainly aware that an economic approach to history was only one, yet dispensable, element in the study of society. Economics is a discipline constructed on the basis of elements of many sciences—geography, biology and psychology—and it interacts with a whole range of subjects from the history of culture to politics, law and religion. Keynes had a very good background in most of these disciplines but it is probably true that he was not sufficiently aware of the connections that certainly exist between the economic and the biological process.

In addition to the scientific law you mentioned, I would like to say that it is crucial to understand the biological basis of human social behavior to shed light on the problem of the origin of society. Man was once defined as a tool-making animal, but now it has been discovered that chimpanzees construct tools designed for particular uses. Neither tools, nor manners characterize man: language does. The invention of a procedure that enabled man to convey information about things not present and to speculate about things not known was the great step. Language made social life much richer and complex and this obviously implies that the economic life of man is much more complicated than that of any other species.

Now, Keynes's dream of a high standard of living for all has been attained in countries such as the United States and Sweden.

---

82. A. Lotka, *Elements of Physical Biology*, Baltimore, 1925.

But, as I point out in one of my books,[83] the change in the scale of values Keynes was pleading for is not in evidence. On the contrary, commercial considerations continue to invade more and more aspects of social life.

D.P.: Now that you have talked about the foundations of economics I would like to present a brief contrast between the epistemological foundations of Keynes's theory and the foundations of his predecessors. In addition to efforts that have been made to contrast the classical and the Keynesian theories[84] from a technical point of view, I think one ought to attempt to understand the methodological differences as well. The problem is not easy given the fact Keynes did not write a book like your *Economic Philosophy*.[85] However, it seems clear that he was influenced to a great extent by the Cambridge group of philosophers of his time (particularly B. Russell and G.E. Moore) and by the elaboration of his *Treatise on Probability*.[86]

I have the impression that Keynes's *General Theory* is a very difficult book because it is the culmination of a very long intellectual process. The reader must be familiar with Keynes's previous writings and not only the *Tract and the Treatise on Money*,[87] but also the *Treatise on Probability* and the *Economic Consequences of the Peace*. I think that Professor Samuelson[88] is wrong when he asserts there is nothing in Keynes's previous writings that will help the reader penetrate the complicated analysis of the *General Theory*. If economics is a discipline suspended midway between Professor Popper's second and third worlds,[89] it is clear that it is important to reconstruct the Keynesian *Weltanschauung*, in particular his epistemological principles. Jevons, Walras, Marshall and Pigou differed in their approaches, but they all followed the Cartesian Dictum of the paradigm of the natural sciences. Keynes

---

83. J. Robinson, *Freedom and Necessity*, London, 1971.
84. J.R. Hicks, "Mr. Keynes and the Classics," *Econometrica*, 1927.
85. J. Robinson, *Economic Philosophy*, London, 1962.
86. J.M. Keynes, "A Treatise on Probability," *Collected Works*, London, MacMillan, 1971.
87. J.M. Keynes, "A Treatise on Money," *Collected Works*, London, MacMillan, 1971.
88. P. Samuelson, "The *General Theory* after Twenty Years," R. Leckacham (ed.), *Keynes's General Theory: Reports of Three Decades*, New York, St. Martin's Press, 1964.
89. K. Popper, *Objective Knowledge*, London, 1972.

considered economics as a moral science and instead of using a historical, micro, deterministic, mathematical and mechanical approach he preferred a historical, institutional, non-deterministic, literary and macro approach. But an important question should be asked: Why did a mathematician end up closer to Kantian and Post-Kantian philosophers (Dilthey, Troelsch), and reject the Cartesian epistemological foundations? I do not know if Keynes followed the debates connected with the differences that can be established between *Die Natur und Kultur oder Geistwissenschaften*. But it is paradoxical that he ended up closer to Shakespeare, Nietzsche and Kierkegaard than to Descartes and Mill!

My hypothesis about this point could be summarized as follows. Keynes developed his ideas about the importance of time in his *Treatise on Probability*; his logic-subjective theory of probability is at the basis of the construction of the liquidity preference theory. Professor Popper[90] has criticized Keynes's interpretation of probability because it does not fit very well into important situations physicists encounter in the realm of quantum mechanics; but the trouble is that one could argue that Heisenberg's uncertainty principle does not introduce so many complications as the notion of pure uncertainty does for economics. In this sense, Popper's own propensity theory of probability could be a better specification than Kolmogorov's traditional axiomatization. One could argue that Popper's contribution is restricted to the natural sciences, whereas Keynes's theory emphasizing degrees of belief is the appropriate one for the social sciences. Keynes's negative attitude towards the application of mathematical techniques to economics could be rooted in the Cambridge tradition, but I think his experience with probability theory throws light on this important matter. On the other hand, I think that Moore's influence on Keynes led him to adopt what he describes as "passionate states of contemplation and a rationalist frame of mind." However, the events in Versailles made him discard the attempt to explain human behavior with mechanistic models. The arguments and behavior of Wilson, Clemenceau and Lloyd George, could not be easily attributed to the Cartesian Logic. When one reads many of the fascinating passages of the *Economic Consequences of Peace*, one feels a major attack is being carried out against abstract thought (in Goethe's sense, let us say).

---

90. K. Popper, *Conjectures and Refutations*, London, 4th edition. 1972.

In short, Keynes's *Treatise on Probability*, his relations with Russell and Moore and his experience as an international negotiator provide very interesting material to reconstruct his method. His previous writings, contrary to Professor Samuelson's opinion, do contribute to the understanding of his *General Theory*.

Professor Robinson: The line of research you have presented is interesting and I am of the opinion it could be fruitful and illuminating to continue to analyze those aspects of Keynes's work.

I agree with you that the *General Theory* is a difficult book because it took Keynes many years to get to his main ideas. It was a long struggle to escape from traditional theory, as he used to describe it. Keynes's intellectual process was a long one, but it was not completed. On the other hand, his *Weltanschauung*, as you call it, varied through time. Take for example his essay "The End of Laissez-faire." In it, he advances serious arguments to show that enlightened self-interest does not always lead to public welfare. He was convinced the capitalist system, if used wisely, was a very efficient machine for raising standards of living and stimulating the process of accumulation of capital. But he saw the system, not as immutable, but as a phase in historical development.

Keynes not only brought time back into economics, but introduced a moral problem. One of the aspects that made the *General Theory* so hard to digest was that it advanced the proposition that private virtues (like saving) could become public vices. Keynes demonstrated, in a very convincing way, that it was not possible to believe in an automatic reconciliation of interests (many times conflicting) into a harmonious whole. As I have said in some of my writings, I do not know if Keynes saved capitalism, but he certainly saved economics as an academic subject. Not only did he reintroduce the problem of judgment (and political economy was born again), but his economic agents cannot predict the future. He operated with real and not abstract human beings. But as I have said, Keynes's view of the relative effectiveness of market forces and collective action varied. Sometimes he talks about the necessity of socializing investment, but in the concluding notes to the *General Theory*, he states that the capitalist system, if managed appropriately, will allocate resources in an efficient way. It is true Keynes paid very little attention to microeconomics and to the theory of value yet he never managed to escape in a complete way from neoclassical economics.

I think you are right when you point out that Keynes was aware that economic life cannot be understood as a rational scheme. In this sense your comment is correct, he was much closer to Shakespeare than to Descartes! Keynes's view of economics was aesthetic; he wanted to eliminate poverty because it was ugly and he wanted to reduce unemployment because it was stupid.

On the other hand, your contrast between Popperian and Keynesian theories of probability is interesting and it could reflect the dichotomy that exists between the natural and the social sciences. Economics is not a natural science. The methods of astronomy and physics, controlled experiments and recurring phenomena, cannot be applied to the study of human beings by human observers. I am not saying economists should abandon the scientific method. They should not jump to conclusions on inadequate evidence, or reason on circular arguments. They must, however, be aware that their subject matter has greater political and ideological content than the natural sciences. As a discipline, economics has to float between metaphysic, moral and scientific statements. Keynes was certainly aware that a good economist should reach a high standard in many fields. As he wrote in *Marshall's Obituary*,[91] a good economist must be in some degree a mathematician, a historian, a statesman, a philosopher, a student of human nature. He used to say that competent economists are very scarce because all these gifts are seldom found together in one human being. He admired Marshall because he did fulfill all these conditions!

D.P.: I think one ought to distinguish between ideological and epistemological propositions. The first refers to the beliefs of a person, whereas the second points to the way an intellectual system is structured.

In this context, I challenged Professor Samuelson's assertion[92] in the sense that mathematics and language are isomorphic, not on ideological grounds but on epistemological ones. Mathematics cannot handle qualitative entities.

Professor Robinson: I think that is a useful distinction. I would agree with you in that language and mathematics are not isomorphic. Two of Cambridge's most important economists, Keynes and

---

91. J.M. Keynes, *Collected Works*, London, MacMillan, 1971.
92. P. Samuelson, "Economics Theory and Mathematics," *A.E.R.*, 1949. D. Pizano, "A Conversation with Professor Paul A. Samuelson," in this book.

Marshall reached that proposition by experience and both of them were mathematicians by training. Marshall used to say that it is not possible to put in mathematics propositions such as: "Queen Victoria was better as a woman than as a queen." But Marshall loved the clarity and precision of mathematics and thus, he decided to use it as his secret vice. He would lock himself up to play with equations once he realized there was no big role for advanced mathematics in economics. Keynes had the same experience. His mind was certainly shaped by his *Treatise on Probability*. Yet his attempt to explain reality, and not just to play with logic, led him to reject the mathematical method. Keynes was very skeptical of econometrics. However, national accounting and statistical testing owe much to him; I don't know what would be his reaction, today, to serious and cautious econometric work. Professor Champernowne, who is well trained in mathematics and who often helps people in the faculty, including myself, with their mathematical exercises, is convinced of Keynes's position.

D.P.: Let me turn my attention to a brief analysis of the impact of Keynesian ideas on the management of the Colombian economy in recent years. L. Currie has suggested a solution to the unemployment problem,[93] which differs from the traditional approaches such as Nelson's[94] model of the exchange-constrained economy and Eckaus's[95] model of dualism. His proposal was the basis for the formulation of a four-year development plan that was adopted by the Colombian government and implemented only up to a certain point but far beyond previous efforts.

A rigorous exercise has to be carried out in order to find out what the main economic effects of the plan were. Consequently, I shall confine myself to a very short and simplified analysis of Currie's theoretical standpoint. In Nelson's model foreign exchange availability is the crucial bottleneck; in Eckaus's model capital is the scarce factor. They recommend, of course, to increase price flexibility, factor substitution and to increase scarce factors. But Currie thinks that it is too difficult to achieve those proposals and so he has suggested an alternative: "Theoretically, the problem could be solved in more or less degree if internal demand could be directed towards a good or bundle of goods and services of mass consumption

---

93. L. Currie, " The Exchange Constraint to Development," *E.J.*, 1971.
94. R.R. Nelson, "A Theory of the Low-level Equilibrium Trap," *A.E.R.*, 1959.
95. R. Eckaus, "Factor Proportions in Underdeveloped Countries," *A.E.R.*, 1955.

whose production would require less imports per dollar of output than is called under existing conditions of demand."

For him, mass housing would provide such a bundle of goods since it would generate employment, and would induce multiplier effects, and thus would stimulate the growth of the economy.

This theory is inspired in the works of Keynes, evidently. But Currie overlooks the fact that the elasticity of supply, which was very high in England when Keynes was writing, is not high at all in countries where one finds all sorts of obstacles and bottlenecks to increase production. I do agree with Currie in that employment generation should be a first priority. But the strategy to deal with unemployment must be designed in such a way to take into account the multiple constraints (technical, physical and institutional) that operate on the supply side.

Currie has been cautious to emphasize the difference between his approach and a Keynesian expansion of aggregate demand. He now associates his strategy with the name of Say rather than Keynes. However, he considers that the most important limitation on growth is the effective limitation of demand at the macro level. The essence of his formulation is the combination of low productivity and idle capacity. He explains his paradoxical position (after all, many people consider him a Keynesian, particularly because of his advice to President Roosevelt) by pointing out that Keynes, misinterpreted Say in maintaining that his law was supposed to guarantee full employment at all times.

According to Currie, Say was interested in trying to go behind the money veil to reveal factors and discover that demand, as a general rule, lies behind and activates monetary demand. But I think it could be argued that Keynes did put Say's law into reverse and that Currie's distinction is not clear.

Professor Robinson: It seems clear to me that unemployment in most developing countries is not due to a deficiency of effective demand, but rather to a deficiency of equipment. Keynesian remedies can be effective as a solution to the problem of under-utilization of capacity, but it is evident they cannot create a capacity that doesn't already exist. In the context of development, unemployed labor should be treated as a potential resource. In the third world one finds many countries that consider unemployed workers to be a great problem and they do not realize that capable men and women are a valuable resource that can contribute something useful to the process of economic growth. The only third world country that has been able to solve the problem of unemployment is China with its policy of "walking on two legs." That is to say, selective investment policies are designed and, while capital accumulation takes place, traditional and modern techniques co-exist (let us say, donkeys and railways).

In regard to Say's law, I would agree that in the classical version it did not imply that there would be full employment at all times, but it did imply that there could not be a general excess of production. Say's law also implies that saving determines the rate of investment. But the amount of saving cannot be independent of the rate of investment. If there is an increase in outlay on investment, then income will rise and that will induce an increase in savings. When Keynes pointed this out, he certainly put Say's law into reverse.

D.P.: The problem of unemployment in developing countries seems to be connected with the choice of techniques. In this context I would like to make a few remarks about the capital theory controversy. But let me first make a general remark on the debate. Would you agree that the main problems of capital theory and neoclassical economics do not really have to do with reswitching, but with problems derived from the concepts of equilibrium, expectation, economies of scale, etc.? In other words, do you agree that the assumption of the absence of multiple switching may be comparatively harmless in relation to other assumptions viewed, from an empirical point of view? You seem to suggest this in your recent article[96] and consequently it is a mystery, why so many eminent professors have spent so much time on it. Is it that empirical plausibility is a minor question in the theorist way of thinking?

Professor Robinson: All controversies should eventually lead to an agreement since the rules of logic and the available evidence are the same for everyone. As I stated in a little book,[97] there are five main reasons why a controversy should start: (i) Because the parties fail to understand each other, (ii) Because someone has made an error of logic, (iii) Because the two parties are making different assumptions, (iv) Because there is no sufficient evidence to clear

---

96. J. Robinson, "The Unimportance of Reswitching," *Q.J.E.*, 1975.
97. J. Robinson, *Introduction to the Theory of Employment*, London, 2nd edition, 1969.

up an empirical question, (v) Because the ideological views of the parties involved are different.

At one point of the controversy Professor Samuelson very honestly admitted he had been mistaken with his attempt to construct what he called a surrogate production function.[98] But the debate continued not on the grounds of logical analysis but on ideological ones. Once the M.I.T. professors give up market prices, they are very worried and conceal their doubts by bluffing. However, there is also disagreement derived from lack of understanding. After I published a recent article,[99] Professor Samuelson replied in a way that demonstrated that he does not understand the distinction between historical and logical time that we were talking about when you pointed out elements of Keynes's epistemological position.

Now, I agree with you in that the empirical importance of reswitching is not the point of the controversy. As a matter of fact reswitching cannot occur in the real world; it occurs in a theoretical system that fails to explain reality. Thus the contribution of this point to the development of economic theory is purely negative. It shows that the definition of capital cannot be independent of the distribution of income.

D.P.: One point that is interesting to discuss in this context is the choice of techniques. Some people think that the logic behind the recommendation of introducing less capital-intensive techniques is affected by the capital theory controversy. But I think that it could be argued that the debate is not relevant to the problem of factor proportions. When one speaks about labor-intensive techniques one is referring to additional investment and not to the existing capital stock.

Professor Robinson: I think the capital theory controversy does shed light on why the approach you suggest does not work. The object of development is not to get to the lowest output per head (generated by the most labor-intensive technique), but to obtain more output per unit of investment. The concept of degree of mechanization, which I explain in the book I wrote with Mr. J. Eatwell,[100] is appropriate in this context. The aim of investment is

---

98. P. Samuelson, "Parable and Realism in Capital Theory: The Surrogate Production Function," *R.E.S.*, 1962.
99. J. Robinson, "The Unimportance of Reswitching," *Q.J.E.*, 1975.
100. Joan Robinson and John Eatwell, *An Introduction to Modern Economics*, New York, McGraw-Hill, 1973.

to reduce the labor cost of particular commodities, by increasing output per head. The choice of projects must be made in terms of future labor saved per unit of current investment. When a planner is faced with the problem of choosing between known techniques, any that gives a lower output per unit of investment and a lower output per man, should be rejected.

D.P.: Turning to another topic, I am at present analyzing commodity models which aim at simulating the dynamics of actual systems that exist in world trade. I have analyzed general equilibrium models, cobweb models, systems analysis models and others. Commodity fluctuations have serious repercussions. Therefore, it is vital to develop theoretical frameworks with high degree of explanatory power so as to illuminate the efforts geared towards stabilization. A major drawback of all these models is that they often assume not only perfect competition, but also perfect foresight. A more realistic treatment of the situation would be to describe some of the markets under consideration as bilateral oligopolies operating in a highly uncertain world. In this context, what use could be made of your book on *The Economics of Imperfect Competition*?[101] Your model does not seem to be appropriate because it rules out the main difficulty of a theory of oligopoly, that is to say, the existence of interlocking decisions. Oligopoly implies interdependence in decision-making, and I think you don't take into account this aspect. The Prisoner's Dilemma situation sheds much more light, but the assumptions behind the Von-Neumann Morgenstern utility concept rule out expectations and surprise. If game theory is used as a simulation technique and not as a tool (it can be shown that certain games are very close to general equilibrium systems and linear programming, but the cooperative ones are far from it), it could be possible to develop a relevant framework or at least one with more explanatory power.

Professor Robinson: *The Economics of Imperfect Competition* received an enthusiastic welcome because at the time it was published (1933), economic theory was very far from real events. I think I was on the wrong track. Dynamic theory, that is to say, the analysis of questions connected with themes such as the theory of employment and the accumulation of capital, are much more important than the elaboration of a theory of value.

---

101. J. Robinson, *The Economics of Imperfect Competition*, London, 1933.

In terms of its contribution to the theory of prices, *The Economics of Imperfect Competition* is a very primitive work. I do not think it would help you in understanding price commodity behavior. The greatest weakness of the theory arises from the fact it fails to deal with time. However, I would also agree with you in that I did not analyze the case of oligopoly, but this omission was not due to the fact I thought it was an unimportant matter, but because I was not able to deal with it.

Finally, I would agree with you in that the theory of games was an important contribution to the understanding of oligopoly, However there is an essential difference between a game with stable and known rules and the struggle for survival in the variable conditions of a free enterprise system.

D.P: I would like to present to you now a brief consideration of Marxist economics. First of all, it has always been paradoxical to me why the followers of Marx continue to insist that their system is the only one that is scientific and all the rest are ideological. I would say that to assert that a system has no value judgments and that it is purely objective is a major value judgment in the field of human studies. On the other hand, as Professor Popper[102] has shown, the criteria of demarcation between a scientific and a metaphysical system are its potential falsification or refutability. Marxism has decided to immunize itself from criticism and thus, it has stagnated. Probably the only work which tried to go further than Marx was Rosa Luxembourg's book (*The Accumulation of Capital*, 1951). But, as we all know, Marxists and non-Marxists rejected her book as well.

A closed and dogmatic system cannot claim to be scientific. It will not evolve unless it accepts the procedure of conjecture and refutation. The system Marx elaborated does shed light, in my opinion, on the way a free enterprise system works. But the conceptual framework is weak on many points as is reflected by the failure of Marx's long-term predictions. Allow me to mention two:

(i) Why did the revolution he predicted for England in the last century not occur? First of all, because Marx's epistemological assumptions are mistaken. He accepted Hegel's historicism uncritically. History is not cyclical (the failure of Spengler's

---

102. K. Popper, *Poverty of Historicism*, London, 1958.

and Toynbee's systems illustrate this point) and history is not predictable. Astronomers can predict eclipses, but social scientists are not in the position to predict revolutions. Secondly, Marx overlooked the impact of education on the structure of society. His analysis is carried out in terms of a struggle between two classes. He did not conceive of the possibility of the emergence of a new class of qualified professionals which do not necessarily have physical capital, but that are well-off in terms of human capital.

This situation implies, among other things, that his prediction of the pauperization of the proletariat has not been reflected by what occurred in the real world where greater learning opportunities leading to increased levels of education resulted in an increase in the productivity of labor which was translated into rising wages.

(ii) The Marxian doctrine of the falling rate of profit, which would lead to a chronic stagnation of the system, has failed as well. I think his philosophical foundations are shaky on this point as well as his empirical observations. Marx assumes that technical progress is of the laborsaving kind and thus, he slips again into determinism, the Hegelian sin! Technical progress is evidently unpredictable. Innovations can be either capital or laborsaving. The Marxist system is based on Ricardian economics and Hegelian philosophy. Both of its foundations have complicated weak points. If Marxism wants to gain the status of a serious school of thought, it must abandon much of its ideological and epistemological principles. As a system it needs considerable reconstruction. After all, Marx was writing during a special period of English history whereas, nowadays we have much greater knowledge about the operation of the international economic system. Everything that has been learnt by social and natural scientists would provide very valuable material for making progress in the analysis of the free market economy. I am convinced that if Marx resuscitated, he would be the first to start his analysis all over again. Nevertheless, his followers have such a degree of admiration for him that they usually do not feel the need to read him, as sometimes happens with the Bible, or in the field of conventional economics with Keynes's *General Theory*.

Professor Robinson: I must start by saying that I believe with Professor Schumpeter[103] that Marx was a great economist. One of his main contributions to the history of thought was to point out the ideological element in the development of the social sciences. But Marxism itself is an ideology, and many of Marx's followers adapted his hypothesis as dogmas. They have treated Marx as a prophet and not as a scientist. By doing this, they drowned the scientific element of Marx's theory in theology. I do agree in that science progresses by trial and error, and when the errors are not recognized, there can be no progress at all.

Marx did put forward testable hypotheses. Let me examine some of the predictions you have mentioned. It appears that Marx's prediction of the increasing misery of workers has not been fulfilled. Marx overlooked the fact that the rise in productivity that capitalism brings about has been sufficient to encourage a dynamic process of accumulation of capital and an improvement in the conditions of living of the workers. When Marxists are challenged on this point they refuse to accept that their master was wrong. They prefer to adopt a dogmatic attitude and, either they deny that real wages have risen, or, they claim that Marx did not put forward that particular hypothesis. The situation is that Marx's powerful analysis has failed here and it is in need of a drastic reconsideration.

The doctrine of the falling rate of profits is very confusing. First, the definition of the organic composition of capital is not clear. It leads to ambiguous repositions. Secondly, as I point out in my *Essay on Marxian Economics*,[104] the law of the falling tendency of profits is in contradiction to the rest of Marx's argument. For, if one assumes with Marx, that the rate of exploitation is constant, real wages should rise as productivity increases.

On the question of Marx's cyclical view of history, I would agree with you in that his concept of stages of history has not proved to be compatible with observation. Socialism has not emerged from the advanced industrial nations. On the contrary, there seems to be a clear connection between the poverty of nations and their propensity to become socialist states. You could be right in pointing out that Marx accepted the Hegelian method uncritically. In my *Open letter from a Keynesian to a Marxist* I point out, in a rather humorous manner, that whenever I discuss a concrete point with a

---

103. J. Schumpeter, *Capitalism, Socialism and Democracy*, London, 12th edition, 1970.
104. J. Robinson, *An Essay on Marxian Economics*, London, 1942.

Marxist, he speaks in "hegelese," a language I don't understand. For example, Marx's definition of constant capital, whether it is a stock or a flow, is very difficult to discuss with a Marxist. They always give you Hegelian explanations and since they take for granted Marx's genius, they do not bother to clear up the matter.

The contribution of Marx to economic theory and to the history of thought was very great. The economic interpretation of history is a fruitful method, that is to say, the interplay of class interests. The Marxian framework needs important adjustments and in this way it provides a powerful attack to the doctrines of the neoclassical school. But without reconsideration it is a source of great confusion.

With reference to Rosa Luxembourg's work, I wrote in the introduction of the English edition that it offers a theory of the process of accumulation of capital of great interest. In many respects, she managed to go beyond Marx (although Marxists rejected her analysis). Take for example the aspect of the influence of geography and climate of a country. Marx never anticipated the great differences of standard of living between North and South America. He did not take into account the influence of climate on human character. Rosa Luxembourg discusses this aspect although she neglects the rise in real wages.

In short, in spite of all its weaknesses, the Marxist approach to economic problems is highly valuable and with careful reconstruction, it can be improved a great deal in the sense that its explanatory power can be increased.

D.P.: Another aspect that causes great difficulties is Marx's theory of value. It has been stated that the celebrated transformation problem has been solved by Piero Sraffa[105] with his invention of an invariable standard of value. However, I think Sraffa's solution is highly hypothetical since he assumes, like Ricardo, uniform rates of profit. As I pointed out to him, in a short conversation a few years ago, the assumption of a uniform rate of profit is incompatible with his famous 1925 article. If increasing returns, uncertainty and oligopoly are considered, it is not clear how a uniform rate of profit will emerge.

---

105. P. Sraffa, *Production of Commodities by means of Commodities*, Cambridge, 1961.

Professor Robinson: The search for an invariable standard of value is based on a false analogy. Length and weight are relations between man and the physical world. Value arises in social situations, that is to say, it is a relation between man and man. Sraffa's solution to the problem is highly artificial, but he made an important contribution. He challenged the concept of the marginal productivity of capital.

With regard to the labor theory of value, I would say that it is grand, political and ideological. It does not assert anything. I tried to show in my *Essay on Marxian Economics* that the labor theory of value is not important at all for the development of Marx's argument. It is only a tautology.

D.P: You have had the opportunity to visit and write about the People's Republic of China. I wonder if you could shed light on some points given that Chinese affairs remain something of a mystery, to say the least:

(i) In one of your books, *Notes on China*, you explain that Chinese people regard the United States as a major threat to humanity. But are they not equally, or perhaps even more, afraid of the Soviet Union? Recent events tend to show that China and the USA are more in the line of cooperation than in the line of confrontation, (ii) What is the attitude of Chinese planners towards the new methods of planning and optimization proposed by people like Professor Kantorovich[106] in Russia which emphasize the efficient allocation of resources and the breaking down of the rigidity of over-centralization? Would you say Chinese planning has been successful in terms of the degree of achievement of the proposed goals? (iii) What is the actual balance between material and moral incentives to increase production? (iv) Is the role of industry in economic development becoming more important? According to a paper written by J. Low[107] the rate of growth of Chinese industry for the last twenty years has been around 7 percent in contrast to only 2–3 percent in agriculture.

Professor Robinson: The Chinese attitude towards the United States and the Soviet Union has certainly evolved through time.

---

106. L.V. Kantorovitch, *Essays in Optimal Planning*, Oxford, 1977.
107. J. Low, "Economic Development and Industrialization," Yuan-Liwu (ed.), *China: A Handbook*, 1973.

There is certainly an atmosphere of tension between the governments of Russia and China.

With reference to the Chinese methods of planning, I would like to say the following. The planners have made a careful study of the Soviet experience in order to learn from its mistakes. They do use some mathematical techniques such as material balances, but the overall objectives are dictated, of course, by the political considerations of the Communist party. There seems to be a problem of disparity of incomes between regions and thus parameters are introduced to reduce this gap. The system is not controlled by any criterion of success, such as profitability, but as the Chinese put it, by the high level of political consciousness of the workers.

With regards to industrialization, the Chinese rejected the Soviet method of extracting the surplus out of agriculture. Chinese planners arrange so that the cultivators have a certain degree of purchasing power. As industrial production develops, the terms of trade evolve in favor of agriculture. Chinese planning has been successful up to a certain point: earthquakes and meteorological catastrophes have made long term planning a very difficult task.

D.P.: To end this interesting conversation, I would like to ask you the following question: What do you consider to be your greatest contribution to economic theory?

Professor Robinson: I regard my *Accumulation of Capital* as my most important work. It is very imperfect of course, but its subject matter is very important. I had to go through a very difficult struggle to write the book. Technical Progress, in particular, is an impossible subject.

D.P.: What were your main intellectual influences in your academic work?

Professor Robinson: My debt to Keynes is obvious in many of my writings. The privilege of having been a member of the group that worked with Keynes while the *General Theory* was being written was very important in my intellectual development. Marx also made a great impact on me, in particular through the eyes of M. Kalecki. Piero Sraffa used to tease me, saying that I treated Marx as a little known forerunner of Kalecki, and in a sense, this was not just a joke. Marshall was also an important influence. But, as I have stated elsewhere, the more I study Marshall, the more I admire him as an economist and less as a human being.

D.P.: What areas of economic theory would you recommend students in developing countries focus on as particularly relevant?

Professor Robinson: I would recommend that they not bother with equilibrium theory and *laissez-faire* policies. The very concept of development is incompatible with the theory of equilibrium and free trade. But economics alone cannot provide the answers of the problems of the third world. The political issues are dominant.

Bibliography

L. Currie, "The Exchange Constraint to Development," *Economic Journal*, 1971.
R. Eckaus, "Factor Proportions in Underdeveloped Countries," *A.E.R.*, 1955.
J.R. Hicks, "Mr. Keynes and the Classics," *Econometrica*, 1937.
J.M. Keynes, *Collected Works*, London, Macmillan, 1971.
———, *Essays in Persuasion, Collected Works*, London, Macmillan, 1971.
———, *A Treatise on Probability, Collected Works*, London, Macmillan, 1971.
———, *A Treatise on Money, Collected Works*, London, Macmillan, 1972.
L.V. Kantorovich, *Essays in Optimal Planning*, Oxford, 1977.
A. Lotka, *Elements of Physical Biology*, Baltimore, 1925.
J. Low, "Economic Development and Industrialization," in Yuan-Uwu (ed.), *China: A Handbook*, 1973.
R.R. Nelson, "A Theory of the Low-level Equilibrium Trap," *A.E.R.*, 1959.
D. Pizano, "A Conversation with Professor Jan Tinbergen," in this book.
———, "A Conversation with Professor John Hicks," in this book.
———, "A Conversation with Professor Paul A. Samuelson," in this book.
K. Popper, *The Poverty of Historicism*, London, 1958.
———, *Objective Knowledge*, London, 1972.
———, *Conjectures and Refutations*, London, 4th edition, 1972.
J. Robinson, "The Theory of Money and the Analysis of Output," *RES.*, October 1933.
———, *The Theory of Imperfect Competition*, London, 1933.
———, *An Essay on Marxian Economics*, London, 1942.
———, "Mr. Harrod's Dynamics," (review) *Economic Journal*, March 1949.
———, *The Accumulation of Capital*, London, 1956.
———, *Economic Philosophy*, London, 1962.
———, *Introduction to the Theory of Employment*, London, 2nd edition, 1969.
———, "Harrod After Twenty-one Years," *Economic Journal*, September 1970.
———, *Economic Heresies*, London, 1971.
———, *Freedom and Necessity*, London, 1971.
———, "The Unimportance of Reswitching," *Q.J.E.*, 1975.
———, "Michal Kalecki on the Economics of Capitalism," *Oxford Bulletin of Economics and Statistics*, February 1977.
P. Samuelson, "Economic Theory and Mathematics," *A.E.R.*, 1949.
———, "Parable and Realism in Capital Theory: The Surrogate Production Function," *R.E.S.*, 1962.
———, "The *General Theory* After Twenty Years," R. Leckacham (ed.), *Keynes General Theory: Reports of Three Decades*, New York, St. Martin's Press, 1964.
J. Schumpeter, *Capitalism, Socialism and Democracy*, London, 12th edition, 1970.
D. Seers (ed.), *The Crisis in Planning*, Edinburgh, 1972.
P. Sraffa, *Production of Commodities by Means of Commodities*, Cambridge, 1961.
T. Swan, "Growth Models of Golden Ages and Production Functions," in *Economic Development*, K. Berrill (ed.), London, Macmillan, 1964.

A Conversation with Professor Paul A. Samuelson

I first encountered Professor Samuelson's textbook, *Economics*, in 1968 and it was the first economics book that I read from cover to cover. It was a good edition, published in Madrid, Spain. I thought it was an excellent introduction to the subject and it greatly influenced my decision to study economics. Samuelson's book made me realize that rigorous analytical methods could be applied to real world problems, that precise methods could be used to arrive at solutions and a greater understanding of important issues. Later, over the years, I had the opportunity of reading and examining several of his works and I was taken aback by the versatile mind of this professor. Original and thought-provoking contributions were to be found in everything he wrote, which, amazingly, ranged from the theory of international trade and the theory of well being to the theory of public finances! As I explained in the prologue to this book, Professor Samuelson was the first scholar who supported this project. I have an enormous debt of gratitude towards him. I visited him in April 1976, at his office at MIT. From his window one could observe several sailboats navigating the Charles River. His mind generated many ideas, and, on occasion, he would use a blackboard in his office to explain an argument mathematically. In October 2007, I visited him again and I was surprised to find him at his 92 years reading the latest economic journals and talking lucidly about many issues.

Professor Paul A. Samuelson from MIT does not need an introduction. It is enough to mention that the Swedish Academy of Science awarded him a Nobel Prize in 1971 for his multiple contributions to diverse areas of economic theory and because he is considered the economist who has most worked to make economics into a science. His complete works include more than 500 technical articles and numerous books.

The Conversation

Diego Pizano: I would like to start this discussion by making reference to a theme that has generated a considerable degree of controversy among economists of different schools: The nature of economic thought. In my opinion it is essential to understand the logical status of economic propositions. But before entering into the analysis of this point, I would like to know your opinion about the necessity or justification of epistemological debates in our discipline. Many economists consider that the place of this discussion in the hierarchical structure of the discipline is at best undefined;[108] in addition they do not believe it is important to study philosophy of science to improve the quality of their hypothesis.

Professor Samuelson: I think most economists, most of the time, do not have to be explicitly aware of methodological questions. Up to a certain point they work as many physicists and biologists I have met, who know nothing explicit about the epistemological aspects of their discipline. They regard with some contempt those who devote a lot of time to these problems and do not search for better hypotheses, which would improve their understanding of nature and the universe.[109] I do not think that every young graduate student who wants to do research needs to devote a lot of time to methodological discussions. I would go even further in saying that, if an economist only talks about these problems, this might be a good indication of his sterility. However, I do not see anything irregular if some people devote a reasonable proportion of their time to this type of study. In my case, I have a certain interest in this area and I do not see the need to apologize to my colleagues for this fact.[110]

---

108. For example, D. Robertson affirms in *Essays in Monetary Theory*, London, 1940: "I must start my defense by saying some words on the unpleasant subject of methodology." Harrod, in turn, warns against the risk of speaking about methodology in his well-known essay, "The Scope and Method of Economics," *Economic Journal*, September 1938.
109. This seems to admit exceptions. Several eminent members of the scientific community such as Sir John Eccles have pointed out that Karl Popper's work in the philosophy of science has deeply influenced the development of their work. See among others, *The Logic of Scientific Discovery*, and *Conjectures and Refutations*.
110. It is interesting to note that Professor Samuelson highlights the need for methodological debates more strongly in the preface of *Foundations of Economic Analysis*, Harvard University, 1947.

D.P.: One of the classical problems of this area is to determine to what extent economic theory has been constructed by inductive or deductive processes, or by a combination of both. I would also like to question Milton Friedman's statement when he says that the realism of the premises of a theory has nothing to do with the validity of its conclusions.[111]

Professor Samuelson: This theme would, of course, require a long analysis. Consequently, I will confine myself to explaining the methodology I am using at this stage of my career. My points of view on this subject have not stayed the same over the course of my academic life because experience has led me to change some of my opinions. However, these changes have not been radical. I consider empirical reality as the guiding fact for constructing scientific theories. In other words, theories do not emerge from our brains as *a priori* Kantian synthetic truths. The fact that nobody can travel at a speed higher than that of light and the fact that an apple and a feather will always fall at the same speed in a vacuum, constitute data from empirical reality. Our theories have to adapt themselves to the facts. Consequently, I would find it absurd to have to choose between induction and deduction. But, if someone were to force me to choose between the two of them at gunpoint, I would have to choose induction.

Deduction is essentially a more prosaic and pedestrian problem of language. Whether you call something poverty or if you call it *pauvreté*, it does not change the nature of the problem. On the other hand, it is very difficult to make inductive inferences. A world jury of wise men would find it difficult to reach a consensus as to the right way of making inferences on the basis of induction. I think there is an external reality which one may try to explain gradually through time. This reality out there is so complicated that no one wants an exact description of all the aspects of the universe. To find out how each leaf falls in the autumn and how it blows would be as complex as reality itself. That is why we are always looking for guiding regularities that will simplify reality and, in that sense, we distort the phenomena we observe. In my opinion a good strategic simplification is very useful.

Because I have stated that I prefer empirical induction rather than theoretical deduction I wish to correct a possible misapprehension.

---

111. See M. Friedman, *Essays in Positive Economics*, Chicago University Press, 1962.

Some people believe that the facts from empirical reality tell their own story. All you have to do is to go out to reality with a blank mind, completely devoid of any previous influence (like an Eastern Kodak film) and the facts will organize in your brain. The German Historical School is to be criticized not because of its interest in facts (classical economists should be criticized because of their lack of interest in empirical reality) but because they believed facts would arrange themselves and tell their own story.

In all sciences there is a debate between those who support Bacon and those who guide themselves by Newton. The former would say that you have simply to collect all the facts and they will organize themselves whereas the latter think you need some model or theoretical hypothesis according to which you understand the facts and rearrange them. It seems to me that not all the fields of knowledge are similar: in the field of celestial mechanics Newton's method was extremely rewarding. On the other hand, if you were studying alloys and you decide to mix copper and zinc you might get an element that is not halfway between them. So there is no substitute for detailed empirical investigations. In short, there is always tension between the Baconians and the Newtonians. What I would like to make clear is that I completely repudiate the opinions of thinkers such as Lionel Robbins and Ludwig Von Mises (and all the Austrian school) who believe in *a priori* truths. My professor Frank Knight believed in them to a certain extent. I think that is a delusion.

I also think that when Friedman says some harmless things he is in agreement with many philosophers of science but he always spoils a good story by taking arguments to the extreme. I do not think an axiom is independent of its conclusions. You are familiar with my ideas on this subject so I will not elaborate this point further. Wong has written a Ph.D. thesis at Cambridge attempting to refute my position but I would not like to make comments on it because I am not sure I have understood his arguments.[112]

D.P.: Some neo-Kantian and post-Kantian thinkers consider a distinction has to be made between the natural and social sciences (*Natur und Kultur Wissenschaften*). One consequence of this distinction is that social sciences cannot follow the epistemological

---

112. See Stanley Wong, "The F-twist and the Methodology of Paul Samuelson," *The American Economic Review*, June 1973.

trajectory of the natural sciences. In this context, the dream of Walras of constructing a model of an interdependent economic system on the basis of his studies of celestial mechanics rests on an analogy that was not adequately justified.

Professor Samuelson: Ludwig Von Mises, who represents an extreme of liberal economics, also considered that distinction valid. He had a brother, Richard Von Mises, a well-known physicist, with whom he had profound disagreements. Richard was a positivist and Ludwig always said that one could not understand human beings in the same way as stones. I think that is an overshot distinction. There is always the aspiration of reaching the prestige of the natural sciences that may lead to an exaggerated and sterile scientism. We are all human and we have a shortcoming: We are fascinated with rigor.

On the other hand, the same was said of biology. Yet all the big advances in this discipline, including the most revolutionary advancement since Darwin—the double helix—were attained by using the method of physics. Crystallography is based on the same epistemological assumptions as physics. If someone constructs a Walrasian type model using the same behavior propensities for a group of altruistic saints and for a group of atomic Friedmanites (who do not care about others) he would be on the wrong track. It would be like using the electromagnetic laws to explain those associated with gravity. They are similar but not identical. I think that what we model in the social sciences is influenced by our imagination. An astronomer cannot ask himself: If I were a star, how would I behave? But if a colleague comes and tells me that an unemployed man would do this or that I can put myself in the situation of that person. Since I am human and I know what it is to be disappointed in life, I can test the realism of the hypothesis. I am taking advantage of this kind of sympathetic introspection and I do not see any reason for not using this procedure. On the other hand, there are problems like the ones that arise in game theory where you get two allegedly omniscient minds with overlapping variables and you get to complex situations that do not exist in a field like quantum mechanics.

There is no reason why some of our problems should be harder than those of the natural sciences and some should be simpler. That still does not make me patient with someone who says that I cannot discuss Marx's transformation problem because I am a well-paid bourgeois economist who knows nothing about sociology and politics. It is obvious that if my knowledge of those disciplines is not adequate it would be difficult for me to discuss the political situation in the Andean countries; but the matrix algebra that is needed to discuss an economy with equal rates of surplus value as against equal rates of profits (markups on everything) is based on logical postulates. Two persons who understand the rules of mathematics should be able to agree easily. I do not think that if 2+2=4 is true in one Kuhnian paradigm and 2+2=5 in another, this is the result of the two persons living in different worlds.[113]

That does not mean that I would use classical mechanics to explain spectral observations in the quantum realm. This realm, in my view, does not violate 2+2=4, nor does the classical. 2×3 is the same as 3×2. But this does not imply that a matrix A multiplied by a matrix B is the same as B×A. Someone might accuse me of abandoning logic. That is not true. It depends on 2+2=4 except that is a different syllogism.

D.P.: Now that you have touched the theme relating to the application of mathematics to economics, I would like to briefly discuss your views on the formal equivalence of mathematics and language.[114] You assert that mathematics is not only a language but you say it is language. How can you demonstrate this isomorphism? My impression is that in certain elemental areas of mathematics you can find a translation of mathematical symbols into literary language but in the area of more sophisticated theorems, for instance in topology, we find ourselves with a set of autonomous propositions (that is to say they correspond to Bertrand Russell's definition of mathematics: "Mathematics may be defined as the subject in which we never know what we are talking about, nor whether what we are saying is true."[115]). In the case of Maxwell's electromagnetic field it would be difficult, if not impossible, to have a clear perception through literary language and vice versa. I do not think that there is a dictionary that would enable us to translate one of Shakespeare's poems into pure mathematics. As you have

---

113. See Thomas Kuhn, *The Structure of Scientific Revolutions*, 2nd ed., University of Chicago Press, Chicago 1970.
114. See P.A. Samuelson, "Economic theory and Mathematics," *The American Economic Review*, May 1952.
115. B. Russell, "Recent work on the Principles of Mathematics," *International Monthly*, 1901.

mentioned, social sciences have tried to match the prestige of the natural sciences and in some cases have adopted excessively rigorous schemes to deal with certain problems which do not admit such sophisticated tools.

I believe that the statements of Descartes and Spinoza in the sense that truth and mathematical proof are identical have reinforced this trend. Coming back to your statement, it seems to me that you are assuming mathematics and language can both be reduced to logic. Consequently, logic is the bridge that would allow the translation from mathematics into language and vice versa. If this was your chain of reasoning, any student of logic would argue that Russell tried to reduce mathematics to logic but his theory of types, which is an essential component of his demonstration, has been severely criticized.[116] In addition, Gödel's conclusion in the sense arithmetic cannot be fully formalized is a great obstacle to Russell's ambition.[117] In short, I do not see how logic can be the vehicle to demonstrate the isomorphism you have proposed.

Professor Samuelson: You cannot discuss logic within logic. Gödel's work has nothing to say about the isomorphism between language and mathematics. Within a logical framework you cannot prove its own consistency.

D.P.: I assume you are referring to Hilbert's work and his propositions about meta-mathematics.[118]

Professor Samuelson: Yes, but that really does not demonstrate the difference between language and mathematics. My opinion is that all the debates that have taken place in the field of mathematical logic (which are very interesting) do not have any power to resolve the debate related to the formal equivalence of mathematics and language.

D.P.: To be absolutely sure I understand your position, do you think Einstein would have been able to develop his special and general theories of relativity without the use of mathematics? In other words, would he have been able to do so with only literary language?

---

116. See, for example, F. Fitch, *Symbolic Logic*, New York, 1952, pp.217–225.
117. For an exposition of Gödel's proof, see E.Nagel, *Gödel's Proof*, *Scientific American*, 1956.
118. *Ibid.*, for an explanation of Hilbert's theories.

Professor Samuelson: Yes. It would have taken him a very long time but in principle it would have been feasible.

D.P.: Now that we are talking about mathematics and economics, do you consider that in order to make progress we need better tools, better assumptions or both? Or what is the main obstacle to improvement?

Professor Samuelson: There are parts of modern economic theory in which the limitation comes from insufficient mathematics. Many of the difficulties of economic theory would not be resolved even if we had another Debreu.[119] The problem, for example, of how any given mixed economy could simultaneously reach a high level of employment, more stable prices and a more equitable income distribution does not need in my opinion a new "tensor" calculus or something of that style. On the other hand, in some areas it could be argued that there are people who are too refined regarding the mathematical techniques they use.

D.P.: Do you consider von Neumann's *Theory of Games* an important contribution to economics? After all, it was the first time interdependence in decision-making was formally introduced in economics.[120]

Professor Samuelson: I think it was an extremely important landmark in the history of economic thought. Certain ancient puzzles were given a good formulation and in a limited set of cases, a solution. Yet his only adequate solution was for two person zero sum games and the majority of the interesting economic problems are not in that format: They are non zero sum games.[121]

---

119. See Gerard Debreu, *Theory of Value: An Axiomatic Analysis of Economic Equilibrium*, John Wiley and Sons, 1959.
120. See J. von Neumann and O. Morgenstern, *The Theory of Games and Economic Behavior*, Princeton, 1944.
121. It is important to highlight two ideas. a) von Neumann considered the general case of a zero sum game involving *n* people, arriving at a series of multiple solutions. Afterwards theoreticians such as Shapely postulated solutions for the game of *n* persons. (See "A Value for *n* Person Games," H.W. Kuhn and A.W. Tucker, eds. *Contributions to the Theory of Games*, Princeton, 1953). *Objective Knowledge*, b) The concept of solution for zero sum games is different and is replaced by standards of behavior.

D.P.: Allow me to go into another theme. Some important economists like Kenneth Arrow and Frank Hahn, have stated recently that the limitations of neoclassical theories are not really related to the problem of reswitching of techniques or to the Cambridge controversies on the theory of capital, but to problems such as the following: (a) The obstacles to incorporate increasing returns to scale. (b) The difficulty of dealing with uncertainty against risk. (c) The lack of an adequate theory to understand the case of oligopoly. Would you agree with this formulation?

Professor Samuelson: To talk about neoclassical theories has certain implications. It is more appropriate to talk about mainstream economics. Otherwise people may think we are postulating one production function for the whole of society and one magnitude you call capital, which can insert into the function and then get useful conclusions about economic policies. It seems to me that in the whole history of economic thought (including schools outside mainstream economics) you cannot find an adequate solution to the problem of uncertainty as different from risk. The problem of oligopoly has also not been solved by any school. Neither the economists of the old Austrian school nor the XXth century Ricardians have solutions to these problems. There are many unsolved problems in economics. I could add other problems to the list you have presented. But from the standpoint of economic policy the most important problem that needs to be solved and which causes a lot of discontent in the life of the average citizen in the United States is the one associated with the simultaneity of recession and inflation: Stagflation. Under which of the three headings you have mentioned would you include it?

D.P.: It seems to be a fourth problem. But I have the feeling it might be connected with the other three. Recession is related to the existence of uncertainty in the minds of investors and inflation might have as one of its causes the oligopolistic structure of some sectors. One would have to build a model.

Professor Samuelson: It could be analyzed in the context of the Arrow-Hahn book, which deals in great detail with market clearing mechanisms.[122] However, those mechanisms are not very relevant

---

122. See K. Arrow and F. Hahn, *General Competitive Analysis*, Harvard University Press, 1973.

for the labor market and that gives rise to certain definitions of unemployment.

D.P.: I would now like to ask you about the contributions of Keynes to economics. I am writing an essay on his thought based on a reading of his collected works. I read your 1946 article and I must say I was somewhat disconcerted because you assert that a mind as great as Keynes was not able to make an original contribution to economic theory. I think Keynes postulated a theory that challenged Say's law and the operation of the invisible hand. He also introduced the tri-dimensionality of time and that, of course, enabled him to go beyond the static equilibrium models. In the light of these remarks, could you clarify your views on Keynes?

Professor Samuelson: This difference of opinion might be semantic and not genuine. I was thinking that pure theory corresponded to the field of microeconomics. One should remember that in 1946 the distinction between micro and macro was not well established. I think he made fruitful contributions, although incomplete, to portfolio theory. The ideas contained in his *Treatise on Money* are very original. If someone argues that not including these contributions in the field of pure theory is a biased opinion, I am willing to modify the wording I used in 1946.

I was not thinking of rejecting those ideas. I was trying to find something similar to Pigou's work that made important contributions to the theory of externalities and welfare economics. In the case of Keynes I found new ideas in the field of index numbers. It is possible that many of those ideas would not exist if he had not proposed them. I found that the support he gave to Ramsey when he prepared his article on savings was important; he also discussed the initial propositions of Sraffa's article. As editor of the *Economic Journal* and as a friend to discuss pure theory his role seems to be more active than what my sentence suggests; but it is very hard to find anything in the field of pure theory. However, if you want to extend the domain of pure theory and state that Keynes found a substitute for Say's law and proposed a new model for understanding effective demand, I would agree. I expressed admiration for those ideas in my article. I also said that his distinction between *ex-ante* and *ex-post* caused a great deal of confusion and triggered a debate that lasted four years in the late thirties. Does saving adjust to investment or vice-versa? This type of question was quite controversial.

D.P.: Allow me to make a reference to the Cambridge controversies on the theory of capital. Joan Robinson has stated that we do not have an adequate theory of capital and we are now going through the second crisis of economic theory (the first one was during the Great Depression) given the fact we do not have a reasonable understanding of the determinants of income distribution. As one of the most active participants of this debate what is your opinion on this statement?

Professor Samuelson: First of all, I must say I have tried to indicate (for instance in my *Economics* textbook) what were the main divergences in the debate. I tried very hard to find in all the writings of Joan Robinson a quotable section about her own theory of distribution and I did not find anything systematic. I can talk about a theory of Kaldor (good or bad) but not about Robinson's theory. She postulates certain golden age tautologies but it is evident she does not believe they explain empirical reality adequately. At the World Congress of the Econometric Society in Cambridge (UK) in 1970, I thought I heard something she said which suggested she did have a theory. She stated that if the workers of Philippines would put political pressure on the supply of labor they could get a higher proportion of GNP. That is a beginning of a theory of income distribution and I thought for two minutes that she did have a theory, but this only underlines the absence of a conceptual framework. I do not know if I am right on this point.[123]

Dobb's last book concludes that we do not have a theory of income distribution. This is a very interesting position for a Marxist economist.[124] After examining the works of Sraffa, Robinson and their opponents and to reach that conclusion is like using a knife that cuts many people, not only J.B. Clark but many others.

In my view, the distribution of income is very hard to change. Whatever the theory is that determines the distribution, it must allow for the fact that if Peron goes into Argentina and as part of power politics of an urban labor movement he raises all money wages by 40 percent, real wages will possibly not increase more than

---

123. Professor Samuelson's criticism seems a bit exaggerated in the light of an examination of the work of J. Robinson. See for example, "The Theory of Distribution," "Capital, Technique and Relative Shares" and other essays on this topic, in J. Robinson, *Collected Economic Papers*, vols. I, IV, Basil Blackwell, 1951–1973.
124. See M. Dobbs, *Theories of Value and Distribution since Adam Smith*, Cambridge University Press, 1975.

6 percent. This does not mean there is a Cobb-Douglas function in a Solow one sector model. I think of the distribution out there as being all too determined. I am not saying it is immutable. I do not believe like Pareto that there is one magic constant that cannot be changed but I think that it very stubbornly resists change.

What is my vision of what causes the system to have that property? The real world is very much like Joan Robinson's *Accumulation of Capital*. There is not just one capital-output ratio, but thousands in each unit of production. Not only can you buy 75 different machine tools from a catalog, but if you had a good reason they would produce a machine that would be halfway between those. The real world has an amazing degree of technological complexity and offers numerous alternatives. Consequently, you need a vector of heterogeneous capital goods. I know I cannot uniquely define time intensity and roundaboutness. Every society known to me, from Mainland China to Western Europe is very far from a golden age (that is to say from an optimal trajectory of growth). In going from any technology that is not optimal to the golden rule, you would maximize the production possibilities for a stationary population. There is an element of truth in the simple old-fashioned parable: You cannot move from a non-golden rule technology to a golden rule technology without a sacrifice of consumption goods. However, the concept is more complicated because if a technology admits re-switching (and this may happen) the transition is not so simple.

For me, China's difficulty to achieve a higher standard of living and a higher life expectancy for its population is not different from what the problem was in 1850 for Western Europe. After 1951, when Joan Robinson started to ask the useful questions I did not insist on the parable mentioned. I admit that reality is more complex and I have learnt something. But it is essentially the same problem. It just takes more sophisticated mathematics to understand its nature.

D.P.: Your statement is very interesting. I think it implies that Harrod-Domar models do not have sufficient explanatory power. Multiple capital-output ratios are not considered in those models.

Professor Samuelson: Evidently, I have never believed that the models of Douglas, or those of Harrod and Domar, or even Solow's improvement, capture reality. On the other hand, when I am in the field of economic policies and I am asked practical questions, as

President Kennedy used to ask me, I find myself using simple models. Is it worthwhile for a society to move from a full employment composition of GNP towards a lower rate of global consumption and a higher rate of capital formation? To answer that type of question I normally use a pragmatic approach. One of the things that Thomas Kuhn did not realize is that a working scientist can use many paradigms simultaneously in his attempts to explain reality and those may be partially inconsistent.

I have a friend who is a good physicist and he tells me that the first time he sees a problem, he uses Bohr's 1913 atomic model.[125] It is not because it is the best model he has, but for a quick first approach is a convenient method. When I do problems, I work with 1936 general theory models and then like a schizoid in a lunatic asylum I move to work in a Walrasian general equilibrium model. If I have a good day I juggle both things and try to find out what combination of those insights is the most useful.

I must confess that the best analysis of what is happening with economic growth and productivity in Western Europe and the United States is Edward Denison's work.[126] In terms of the Cambridge controversies on the theory of capital and the debate between Solow and Garegnani, it is clear that his model is not far from the 1928 untenable and oversimplified Paul Douglas model. If somebody brings me a better model I would be willing to accept it. I think that the studies of Bergson, based on the application of this model to the Soviet Union, represent the best approximation to that reality I know.[127] One of the most surprising findings is that the residual factor, which represents technical progress, is very small. That means that economic growth is basically explained by capital formation, a paradox in the land of the labor theory of value! Bergson uses his model to predict that the rate of growth of the Soviet Economy in the seventies and eighties will not be as high as the one registered in the fifties and sixties because of political constraints: People want to work less and consume more and will decrease the rate of capital formation. Without a new Stalin the system cannot repeat its past performance. That does not imply I

---

125. Böhr is considered the scientist that constructed the modern vision of the atom. His theory consists of an effort to integrate the work of Rutherford and Max Planck (quantum theory).
126. See E. Dennison, *Why Growth Rates Differ*, Brookings Institute, 1971.
127. A. Bergson, *Planning and Productivity under Soviet Socialism*, Columbia University Press, 1968.

would use the concept of surrogate capital in a theoretical analysis.[128] It would be similar to a Marxist using identical rates in the organic composition of capital.

D.P.: I assume you are referring to Garegnani's article on the convexity or concavity of the frontier of factor prices.[129]

Professor Samuelson: Yes. But there is another relevant point of the debate that is called the Hahn problem, although it is older than him.[130] Suppose that the people always save 20 percent of the national income. If you are in a one sector, one capital good Solow model, there is no problem in using those savings given the fact that they would enter the system as capital formation. But suppose we have two or more capital goods or thousands of heterogeneous capital goods as in the real world. In this case, what criteria are used to decide about the composition of the new capital generated by the flow of savings? Hahn thought that efficiency was the answer in the sense of choosing those capital goods, which once selected, would take the process to a situation in which the possibility of regretting that decision would not exist. But the problem is that there is an infinite number of those solutions, a conclusion which requires the use of a very abstract model but which is correct. The conditions of inter-temporal efficiency or the conditions needed to exclude unforeseen capital gains lead to infinite alternatives in a given number of periods. Joan Robinson has pointed out in this context that we do not have an appropriate theory of inter-temporal prices. Someone could argue that if we had perfect futures markets we could find a system of prices that would clear the market indefinitely.

D.P.: Is this the line of argument developed by Hicks in his book *Value and Capital* when he works with a sequence of equilibrium situations through time?

Professor Samuelson: To a certain extent yes, but I do not think that Hicks deals with all the intricacies of the problem. The truth

---

128. See P. Samuelson, "Parable and Realism in Capital Theory: The Surrogate Production Function," *Review of Economic Studies*, 1961.
129. P. Garegnani, "Heterogeneous Capital, the Production Function and the Theory of Distribution," *Review of Economic Studies*, 1970.
130. F.H. Hahn, "On Sector Growth Models," *R.E.S.* 1965; and "Equilibrium Dynamics with Heterogenous Capital Goods," *Q.J.E.*, 1966.

is that we do not have futures markets for all goods (and in very few cases they go beyond 24 months); in addition we do not have constant returns to scale in all sectors and transaction costs are significant. My honest opinion is that the imperfectly competitive system, including bankruptcy, is always redefining itself and we rarely have accentuated business cycles in the United States. It is possible that under a system of checks and balances and with the government acting as an arbiter, a solution could be found which would not be too far from the theoretical optimum. These actual movements of economic history are not very far from the trajectory suggested by dynamic programming. This assertion is based, not on a singular econometric study but on all my observations and that is why I would be willing to defend my thesis as Galileo did during the Inquisition.

D.P.: I have the impression that the Soviet Union is giving increasing attention to market simulations in order to search for consistent solutions in its long run plans. It seems paradoxical but one can observe a trend, for instance in the works of Kantorovich, towards a convergence with equilibrium postulated by dynamic programming.[131]

Professor Samuelson: It is also interesting to note that if one examines the works of outstanding economists from Russia, Poland and Czechoslovakia and one compares them with the models of some rather reactionary mathematical economists from the USA, the degree of convergence is much higher than the one that exists with the more radical thinkers. Of course the speakers of this last group would say: But who has said that Russia and their satellites are really communist?

D.P.: Schumpeter arrived at the conclusion in his book *Capitalism, Socialism and Democracy* that the coming of the socialist system was inevitable, in spite of the fact he did not think that was desirable. Do you consider this point of view as valid?

Professor Samuelson: Let me tell you an anecdote on this point. There was a famous debate between Paul Sweezy and Schumpeter at Harvard before the war on the future of capitalism. These two

---

131. L.B. Kantorovich, *The Best Use of Economic Resources*, Moscow, 1959.

academics were very good friends. Leontieff was the moderator and he summed up after the debate as follows: both agree that capitalism will die but they disagree on the causes. Sweezy asserts that it is dying of cancer, that is to say, because of its own contradictions. Schumpeter has said that it is dying for psychosomatic reasons in the sense the success of the system is killing it, in the same way a very rich man may be weakened by ulcers and neurosis. Schumpeter mentioned Sweezy, who was the son of a very successful New York banker, as the perfect example of the affluent children turning against the system. I was present at that debate and I consider that Schumpeter was wrong when he thought there is a timetable for the disappearance of capitalism and that there is a progression in which socialism is the final stage. I think that the Victorian capitalism of Herbert Spencer will not last very long but the system has many directions to go different from old-fashioned socialism. Schumpeter never demonstrated in a rigorous way that the success of the system would undermine it. When an economic system operates in a successful way it offers many choices to the members of its society. It gives them more free time, which they can use, for example in analyzing how to improve the system. Schumpeter argued that there was a particularly hateful characteristic of capitalism and that was its excess of rationality and efficiency that could destroy the mythical and the religious. There might be some element of truth in this but it is really a very complex theme.

D.P.: In this context, it is interesting to mention that Keynes argued in one of his essays that economic growth was not an end in itself but a means to initiate a more civilized life. The time devoted to solving the individual economic problem would be minimal and most activities would be oriented towards the moral and spiritual growth of mankind.

Professor Samuelson: Yes, but he also said that we may all experience a collective nervous breakdown. We are so used to the struggle that in its absence many people might become desperate. Durkheim's work and the high suicide rates in some high-income countries give some support to that thesis. But it is certainly premature for a large part of the world. It might have some application in Scandinavian countries and possibly Kuwait. In the United States, the mental health studies I am familiar with point out that the affluent show less signs of mental disease than low-income people. It is possible that the descendants of the Rockefeller family, according to a new book, might be an exception.

D.P.: Before we end this discussion, I wanted to make some remarks on the economic and commercial relations between the United States and Latin America. First of all, there is a paradoxical element with the doctrine of free trade. The vast majority of economists who teach at American universities defend free trade vigorously but when they or their students work for the government, some of them become somewhat protectionist. How can one explain this transformation? On the other hand, I have the impression that Latin American countries are becoming efficient producers of some manufactured goods such as shoes and textiles. However, many of these types of goods do not have free access to the American market. According to recent documents of the U.S. Department of Labor, the American economy is becoming a service economy and the proportion of the labor force working in the manufacturing sector is declining. Dr. Kissinger visited several Latin American countries (including Colombia) recently and he reiterated his thesis about the economic interdependence of this hemisphere; in this context, it would be interesting to explore the possibility of having more trade and more open markets in our hemisphere taking into consideration that Latin American countries are important clients of U.S. capital goods and that they are also supplying valuable primary products at reasonable prices.

Professor Samuelson: The inconsistency criticism might be applicable to businessmen who only support free trade when it is convenient to their enterprises. But most academics in this country are free traders and, sometimes, naively so.

D.P.: I insist that some academics, for instance, attack international commodity agreements and at the same time defend support prices for American farmers. Is this not an inconsistency?

Professor Samuelson: I would be prepared to believe that given the fact economists are human they are sometimes inconsistent. In my own personal case, I have presented some ideas on a trade policy for the United States, which deviate slightly from the solutions derived from pure theory. In a speech I gave in Stockholm before I got the Nobel Prize,[132] I said that according to some U.S. experts this country is losing its comparative advantage in the production of manufactures whereas commercial agriculture remains competitive.

The U.S. economy could become an economy dominated by services as the State of Colorado has become. American multinationals could carry out their manufacturing activities in other countries. Is this scenario only possible in a free trade world where property rights are respected and expropriations and retaliations do not exist? The political factors make me think it is difficult to apply this free trade model at the world level but I do not think I should be criticized for having this opinion. On the other hand, I have criticized some of Dr. Kissinger's economic ideas. In the case of the world oil market, for example, I was in disagreement with his proposal of establishing a minimum and a maximum price. I argued that the floors would have legal meaning whereas the ceilings would not. Finally, I would like to say that the problem of many economists is that they do not make their recommendations viable because they ignore the political constraints.

D.P.: In other words, would you agree that the study of economics cannot be reduced to training people in mental acrobatics but that it should be oriented towards solving real world problems?

Professor Samuelson: I fully agree. The difficult battles are the ones associated with understanding the complexity of reality.

---

132. P. Samuelson, "International Trade for a Rich Country," Swedish American Chamber of Commerce, 1971.

Bibliography

K. Arrow and F. Hahn, *General Competitive Analysis*, Harvard University Press, 1973.
A. Bergson, *Planning and Productivity under Soviet Socialism*, Columbia University Press, 1968.
G. Debreu, *Theory of Value: An Axiomatic Analysis of Economic Equilibrium*, John Wiley and Sons, 1959.
E. Dennison, *Why Growth Rates Differ*, Brookings Institute, 1971.
M. Dobbs, *Theories of Value and Distribution since Adam Smith*, Cambridge University Press, 1975.
F. Fitch, *Symbolic Logic*, New York, 1952.
M. Friedman, *Essays in Positive Economics*, Chicago University Press, 1962.
P. Garegnani, "Heterogeneous Capital, the Production Function and the Theory of Distribution," *Review of Economic Studies*, 1970.
F.H. Hahn, "On Sector Growth Models," *R.E.S.* 1965; and "Equilibrium Dynamics with Heterogenous Capital Goods," *Q.J.E.*, 1966.
L.V. Kantorovich, *The Best Use of Economic Resources*, Moscow, 1959.
T. Kuhn, *The Structure of Scientific Revolutions*, 2nd ed., University of Chicago Press, Chicago 1970.
E. Nagel, Gödel's Proof, *Scientific American*, 1956.
J. Robinson, *Collected Economic Papers*, vols. I, IV, Basil Blackwell, 1951–1973.
B. Russell, "Recent work on the Principles of Mathematics," *International Monthly*, 1901.
P.A. Samuelson, *Foundations of Economic Analysis*, Harvard University, 1947.
———, "Economic theory and Mathematics," *The American Economic Review*, May 1952.
———, "Parable and Realism in Capital Theory: The Surrogate Production Function," *Review of Economic Studies*, 1961.
———, "International Trade for a Rich Country," Swedish American Chamber of Commerce, 1971.
J. von Neumann and O. Morgenstern, *The Theory of Games and Economic Behavior*, Princeton, 1944.
S. Wong, "The F-twist and the Methodology of Paul Samuelson," *The American Economic Review*, June 1973.

A Conversation with
Professor Jan Tinbergen

All economists that have passed through graduate school have encountered the important writings of Professor Jan Tinbergen (1903–1994). His econometric work on economic cycles has been well known since the thirties. His essays and books on the theory of economic policies and on development were widely read during the sixties and seventies. When in Cambridge, I spent many fruitful hours reading the *Complete Works of Keynes*. There I was to find many of the letters exchanged between these two great masters of economic thinking. All these reasons led me to think that this renowned economist had a lot to contribute to this book. I wrote to him in early 1977 when I was at Oxford, explaining this project. A few days later he answered, inviting me to his home. So it was at his pleasant house in The Hague, Holland in his personal library that we were to talk. Upon entering his residence he greeted me by telling me that an ex-President of Colombia, Carlos Lleras, had invited him to his inauguration in August 1966, which he was unable to attend because of an excessive number of international engagements. Nevertheless, he told me that he was very interested in matters relating to the economic development of Latin American countries. He had the humility that characterizes the truly wise, and he was particularly cordial and kind.

At the time this dialogue took place, in April 1977, Doctor Tinbergen was Emeritus Professor at the University of Rotterdam. In his youth he had finished a Doctorate in Physics and on various occasions had the opportunity of talking to Professor Albert Einstein. Later, he turned to Economics as a reaction to the Great Depression of the thirties. He was the Director of the Planning Office for Holland, and President of the UN Planning Committee. He was recognized as one of the founders of econometrics, empirical macroeconomics, the theory of economic policy, and the theory of economic development. He published more than ten books and over two hundred articles in specialized journals. The Swedish Academy of Science awarded him the first Nobel Prize in Economics in 1969 in recognition of his contributions to the field. The same year his brother, Nicolas Tinbergen, received the Nobel Prize in Medicine, a rather unusual event.

The Conversation

Diego Pizano: It would be interesting to start by commenting on some methodological problems relevant to the evolution of economic thought and the relations between the construction of economic theory and its application. I am aware that in talking about these matters we would be venturing into the realm of philosophy, but I am convinced economists should be aware of the nature of their subject and the epistemological problems connected with its foundations. A useful basis for treating these questions could be the analysis of Keynes's[133] reaction towards your work on statistical testing of the theories concerned with the explanation of business cycles.[134] I think that Keynes's arguments could be summarized in two propositions:

(i) Multiple correlation is not an adequate method because the economic material is not homogenous through time.
(ii) He pointed out that you were assuming a determinate function of past statistics. What place is left for expectations and the state of confidence relating to the future?

The crucial question seems to be: To what extent should economics follow the methods of physics? It should be taken into account that the number of significantly connected variables seems to be much larger in economics while economic relationships are not as stable to the degree they are in physics.

In terms of the second question, it concerns the role that confidence and expectations play in terms of the future. It would be very interesting to hear your views on these questions forty years after your exchange with Keynes.

Professor Tinbergen: I think I understand your question. Keynes certainly indicated some difficulties with econometric methods but I haven't changed my attitude in principle. I still feel that the

---

133. J.M. Keynes, *Collected Works*, Royal Economic Society, vol. XIV, pp. 285–320, 1973. See correspondence between Keynes and Tinbergen and between Keynes and Harrod.
134. J. Tinbergen, *An Econometric Approach to Business Cycles Problems*, Paris 1937.

method used by physics has applicability outside its domain. I agree that in some cases relevant phenomena, such as expectations, have not been measured and, of course, were not measured at that time. But we substituted elements that we thought would come close to them. Normally we call these "dummies." One example is that in some speculative markets one can estimate expectations about the future price by simply extrapolating the movements of the last few weeks or months depending on the commodity in question. In other cases you could make enquiries asking people explicitly for their expectations.

These remarks bring me to my main point of agreement with Keynes: in order for a multiple correlation to be an adequate method you must include the relevant phenomena. Not necessarily all the events associated with the problem must be included but certainly the relevant ones. Unless you have them, the multiple correlations are not worth much. But you can, over the course of time, having discovered that some events are relevant and yet haven't been measured, attempt to measure them. In that respect I think like a physicist. After all, I have been educated as a physicist, and I do believe in the possibility of even measuring things that others have singled out as non-measurable. In principle, I think that one can always attempt to measure. I would even add that the progress that can be made in any science is dependent on one's willingness to make measurements since the rejection of a theory can most convincingly be made after you have tried to measure the phenomena and get a negative result.

D.P.: Would it be correct to say, according to your statement, that economics and physics are faced with the same kind of problems? Because in addition to Keynes's position (economics is a moral science and not a natural science) one can find an interesting alternative proposed by people like von Neumann. He used to say that the problem with the application of the physicists' mathematical models was that they had not been designed to meet the difficulties of typical social problems encountered in economics. In other words, social problems were different in kind and in degree according to his views. For example, the problem of oligopoly where you find a situation in which various minds intersect each other and so mutual interdependence in the selection of strategies is a crucial element. This type of situation does not seem to exist in classical mechanics or in the more recent developments of quantum mechanics. That was the reason why von Neumann had to invent a new set of mathematical tools that could cope with that sort of problem. In conclusion, would you accept that some of the problems economists have to face do not have a counterpart in physics and consequently the analogy won't always work?

Professor Tinbergen: Certainly, that is quite true. Just to mention the most evident fact, physics does not have to deal with living beings. This implies the possible necessity of introducing concepts in economics that are not known in physics. Moreover, I would like to come back to one of the remarks you made before. I do agree with you when you say that the number of variables playing a role in economic phenomena is very large and that is an additional difficulty. I could also say that the stability of relationships is not always certain and consequently one must test theories continually. If a theory is rejected, one has to try another one. I think that for this reason one has to change theories more often in economics than in physics although in the latter one can find examples of theories being discarded as in the case of the theories of light. In conclusion, I prefer to speak of a difference in degree although there is no clear-cut frontier between differences in degree and qualitative differences. It is almost a question of taste. It's true that Von Neumann tried to develop quite innovative methods, and game theory is a most interesting attempt. I agree that there are some important possibilities in it that have been hardly explored. On the other hand, I do consider that the older parts of economics can still be used with reasonable success.

D.P.: The subject we have discussed is closely connected with another controversy, and that is the applicability of mathematics in economic theory. As you know, Alfred Marshall believed that it was obvious, and he was a mathematician by training, that there is no room in economics for long chains of deductive reasoning. One could say that the main justification for the use of mathematics in any field is its efficiency as a method of analysis. But can this argument of efficiency be applied in all cases? Or would you say that in some fields, verbal logic and literary analysis would do a better job, for example, in the problem of formulation of economic policies?

Professor Tinbergen: I would not exclude this possibility beforehand. I have a very good recollection that, indeed, I met with situations in which a mathematical treatment did not really help much. Nevertheless, I would say that, in general, whatever can be approached with mathematics can also be translated into verbal statements. It's mostly a question of language and mathematics is a language. In the large majority of cases the mathematical method makes it easier to get a sense of an author's ideas and to force him to be quite sharp in his definitions. In an attempt to conclude this issue I would say that mathematical analysis and verbal logic are essentially equivalent but, in a number of cases, the former is not really necessary or is a bit artificial.

D.P.: From what you just said I don't know whether you would agree with Professor Samuelson's point of view when he asserted that mathematics and language are equivalent.[135] In the discussion I had with him[136] I disagreed with him on this point because I think that, apart from the problems one encounters in the literature on the philosophy of mathematics, mathematics can only handle objective quantifiable entities.[137] The qualitative subjective elements are very hard to incorporate in a model that assumes sharp definitions, uses the axiomatic method and strict interdependence between variables.

Professor Tinbergen: I must confess that I am very close to his point of view. In that respect I might differ in opinion with you. I think that qualitative elements, and that is a term you have introduced, can be represented by a mathematical symbol. This does not imply that it can be measured directly. Whenever we introduce a concept in a qualitative way we can still, if we want to, represent that same concept by a symbol. That would not add too much to the performance of the system but one could change, on further exploration, a qualitative concept into a quantitative one.

My favorite example is one taken from physics, again, and refers to temperature or to what used to be called heat. It was then often maintained that heat was just something that you could feel. You put a hand in water and you would describe it as hot or warm, etc., and it took some time until, almost by coincidence, it appeared possible to introduce the concept of temperature.

---

135. P.A. Samuelson, "Economic Theory and Mathematics," *A.E.R.,* May 1952.
136. D. Pizano, "A Conversation with Professor Paul A. Samuelson," in this book.
137. Gödel's proof, Hilbert's mathematics, etc.

How was it introduced? It was introduced by the observation that if you incorporated heat into the environment, most substances would change volume and, in most cases, in a proportional way. I underline, in most cases, and not in all cases. So one could say it was by a majority vote between various materials that we invented the thermometer. However, it was not by unanimity among all the materials that the thermometer could be constructed because at every temperature, there are some substances that do not increase their volume proportionately to others. This is true, for instance, for the well-known interval of 0 degrees and 4 degrees for water where it does not expand but on the contrary it shrinks. It is also true for any substance that changes its state of global aggregation, when a substance changes from a solid to a liquid or a liquid to a gas; and different substances have different melting and boiling points. So the interesting point is that even in physics, it was very useful to introduce a concept that was not supported by the unanimity of voters. This illustrates a type of uncertainty that is more frequent in the social and the human sciences which means that we have to satisfy ourselves with a lower degree of exactitude than the one we can afford in physics. In that respect there is again a difference, but I would be inclined to call it a difference of degree and not one of quality.

D.P.: When I was thinking of qualitative elements I was thinking of the kinds of problems that arise when making decisions under uncertainty and differences in risk. This means that in many situations economic agents have no way of predicting the future course of the relevant variables of their environment. In other words, the condition of perfect foresight that is postulated by many models is not applicable. The theorist is faced in this situation with the problem of allocating an objective probability to a degree of belief that is in fact a subjective probability. Now, you can ask the economic agent to order his degrees of belief but he will be able to do it in a qualitative way, and not in a quantitative one. I think no school of economic thought has been able to solve this problem. And I would say that not even physics has done so after Heisenberg postulated his uncertainty principle. One can find many stock markets and future trading markets where degrees of belief and expectations play a very important role.

The situation brings the complications associated with the paradoxes of time. Even though Bertrand Russell stated that the mathematical continuum could help understand the concept of time, people like Poincaré concluded that not even Cantor's celebrated theory of transfinite numbers had power to solve the mystery of time. Given the previous considerations, I don't know to what extent expectations in economics can be made analogous to the problem of temperature you were talking about. Or is it a different problem that seems to be more complicated?

Professor Tinbergen: Well, let's perhaps agree that there are a number of difficulties close to the ones you have set out. I am not at the moment able to make a very precise statement here. I would like to select another case that could illustrate your own point even though it is not exactly the same.

I do agree that there are, especially when one is faced with the problem of applying economic science to decision making, a number of so called subjective elements, or value judgments. We, as economists, now generally agree that there are a number of value judgments without which we cannot solve certain problems of economic policy. Here I certainly follow my Swedish colleague Gunnar Myrdal who not only states this fact, but adds that the way out is that each author whenever discussing such an issue must explicitly mention his value judgments. I would like to add an example here on the subject that has been close to my thought these last few years connected with utility functions or welfare functions. I think I can illustrate my case by stating that to try to find the welfare function of an individual is an objective problem, which is a problem without a value judgment. Your assignment is then simply to find out what the ordering of the preferences of the various possible states of the individual are. But as soon as you start speaking about a social welfare function the element of value judgment comes in. Then I do agree with Myrdal in that, whatever you are talking about, you have to mention it explicitly and all that you are deriving from it depends on whether it is in agreement or not with your value judgment.

D.P.: I would like to take advantage of this opportunity to ask you about your methodology for constructing social welfare functions. In your paper about the theory of the optimum economic system[138]

---

138. J. Tinbergen, *Some Suggestions on the Theory of the Optimum Regime*, Rotterdam, 1960.

you have proposed a way of aggregating individual welfare functions in order to get the social welfare function. I have been examining your method in the light of Arrow's impossibility theorem,[139] which is based on explicit value judgments, and I have a feeling that your procedure would violate some of his conditions. Would you agree?

Professor Tinbergen: Presumably, yes and, in fact, I have a preference here for making things much simpler by starting from the assumption that individual welfare can be measured and all depends on this. This is my simplifying assumption. Of course, it is not clear at all how many economists would subscribe to it. I am in favor of a strategy that simplifies matters and I do agree that if one denies the possibility of comparing the welfare of different persons then a number of well-known difficulties come up. My own attempt is a quicker way to get results and I am aware of the relativity of this position.

D.P.: I would like to conclude this section with a discussion devoted to meta-economic questions. We could say that there are a number of important differences between economics and physics. To what extent should the differences between the social and the natural sciences lead us to consider a special educational program for economists that would include disciplines connected in some way to philosophy, psychology, sociology, ethnology, ecology, history, politics, and not just mathematical techniques? Von Hayek has stated very clearly that in order to be able to make the transition from economic theory to economic policy one has to have a multidimensional training.[140] What is your opinion about this point, which seems to be very important for the design of educational programs?

Professor Tinbergen: In a general, I agree, but for practical reasons we must of course limit ideals. An economist must have some knowledge, indeed, of all those disciplines you mention, but it is next to impossible to be so knowledgeable. That is why cooperation between scientists of different areas is so important. This is what we normally call a multidisciplinary approach. In practice it

---

139. K.Arrow, *Social Choice and Individual Values*, Yale, 1963.
140. F.Von Hayek, *Philosophy, Politics and Economics*, London, 1965.

will often take the form of cooperation between people of different backgrounds. Among them there may be an economist but also sociologists, technicians, psychologists and, in order for them to understand each other, they must have some knowledge of each other's subjects. So I would agree with you that in the education of any of these people some basic knowledge about some of the other subjects that are neighboring his own subject is indispensable. Otherwise he won't be able to cooperate.

D.P.: On this question of multidisciplinary research I would like to ask you: To what extent does the research done by ethnologists like K. Lorenz[141] and your brother, Nicolas Tinbergen,[142] shed light on the problem of economic growth in our planet? In a recent article Professor N. Tinbergen pointed out that cultural evolution and technological progress have already begun to produce an extremely complex set of negative feedbacks. He asserts that our species is in a phase of disadaptation, of loss of viability and that many psychosocial stressors and psychosomatic diseases like asthma, coronary thrombosis and all those are appearing as a result of the atmosphere created by industrial and post-industrial society. The obvious question in connection with economics seems to be: To what extent economists should take into account the biological basis of human social behavior when they formulate development plans which could imply exponential growth of cities, over-competitiveness, etc.?

On the other hand, K. Lorenz in a recent book states that our civilization is in a process of progressive decay and since society is the most complex of all living systems it is imperative to use every discipline to understand its functioning.[143] He is convinced that the problems of our civilization are pathological in nature and thus it has become a necessity to employ the methods of medical science and interpret the findings of etologists. In conclusion, shouldn't we try as economists to take into account the efforts that have been made to reconcile the conflicts that arise between culture and technology and recognize that there are limits to growth at

---

141. K. Lorenz, *On Aggression*, London 1966; *Evolution and Modification of Behaviour*, Chicago 1965; *Studies in Animal and Human Behaviour*, London, 1970; *Civilized Man's Eight Deadly Sins*, London, 1974.
142. N. Tinbergen, *The Study of Instinct*, 1969; *Social Behavior in Animals*, London, 1965.
143. K. Lorenz, *Behind the Mirror*, London 1977.

the medico-biological level? Or should we believe in man's great capacity for adaptation and disregard these alarms?

Professor Tinbergen: I do think that it is a very important problem. The trouble is that quite a bit of information that we need to arrive at some sort of preliminary crude solution is still lacking. In a way, I have acted as a messenger of my brother among my fellow economists and I have said to them to be careful because there may be a danger. In that respect, I am much more cautious than men like W. Beckermann[144] or H. Kahn[145] whom I find too optimistic. Another example about the same subject is the following. Not so long ago a study was made by my countryman, Professor H. Linnemann,[146] about the possibilities of feeding the world population around the year 2010 or so when the present population (using 1970 population as a basis) will have doubled.[147] As an introductory essay to that publication, a study was made by a group of agronomists and experts on geology and climate and they have estimated the total or maximum capacity of the earth to produce food. They have arrived at a figure of thirty times the production of 1970. It so happens that this ceiling did not play any role in the projections of economic growth since long before we would have to face constraints of a social character.

I have very much emphasized the need to critically consider this study that leads to the figure of thirty times and, especially, to find out what environmental difficulties would arise if that production was attempted and attained. So a small group here in the Netherlands has prepared a little preliminary report where it is indicated what factors should be studied further and in what sense that original introductory study would have to be improved and deepened, so that we would be better aware of certain limitations that we simply don't know. To summarize, I do recognize many of the dangers that my brother has indicated, but I do have to add that etologists are often unable to make worldwide estimates

---

144. For a review of Beckermann's book, see D. Pizano, *Coyuntura Económica*, October 1975.
145. H. Kahn, *The Next 200 Years*, London 1977.
146. H.Linnemann,(ed.), *Model of International Relations in Agriculture*, Amsterdam, 1976.
147. World population in 1970 was 3.7 billion people. In 2010 it is expected to be around 7 billion which implies an increase of 89% and not 100% as projected in 1970.Nevertheless, in recent years supply constraints on food production have appeared and food prices have increased.

that would indicate the magnitude of the problem. Let me give an example: They maintain that certain areas must be left in natural conditions. You may call them a sort of gene reserve and this is probably correct. Yet they are not able to tell us which part of the world should be preserved in that way. This is one example of a lacuna where many more data will have to be collected to enable us to be better aware of where, exactly, we stand.

D.P.: Am I allowed to infer that we have limits to growth derived from scarcity of raw materials and, also, limits derived from social and political factors? Would you say that economic growth is only a means to facilitate human spiritual progress and so that beyond a certain point it hasn't got too much justification? I am thinking of utopias like the ones Keynes had in mind when he wrote his essay on the economic possibilities for our grandchildren. He wrote that compound interest and technical progress would increase the general standard of living so much that the economic problem would just disappear and people would devote their time to cultivating themselves in a spiritual sense. The idea appears to be highly desirable, but if one looks at the studies about how people in rich countries use their leisure time and if one combines that with all the constraints we have been talking about, one is forced to conclude that Keynes's ideal was utopian. Would you agree?

Professor Tinbergen: My impression is that I simply don't know. I tried to express this idea in my farewell lecture at the University of Rotterdam when I attempted to answer the question: Will we have a post-economic period? I simply don't know. All I can say is that I see so much social pressure accumulating at present that I can very well imagine that we cannot reach that utopia that Keynes was talking about. On the other hand, it is still a possibility and the optimists I mentioned like H. Kahn and W. Beckermann seem to be convinced that we will get there. It all depends on certain sets of figures, some of which are lacking and so it is very difficult to make a long-term prediction. Intuitively I am not very optimistic in comparison with Keynes or Kahn and Beckermann.

D.P.: I think that the question we are discussing is closely connected with the energy options. The Kahn report, as you were pointing out, is fairly optimistic in that respect. On the other hand, last week President Carter announced his decision of stopping the construction and promotion of nuclear plants, especially in the developing world. It would not be an exaggeration to say that this is one of the most important political issues of our time. Now, it is difficult to assess, at this moment, if Carter's decision will be considered wise in the long run. Experts, such as John Berger, have been warning the industrial powers of the dangers associated with increasing the chances of nuclear war, with the irreversibility of radioactive contamination and the genetic threat to our species.[148] The obvious question: How feasible is the introduction of the so-called clean energy alternatives in the short and medium term? Solar power, geothermal power, wind and ocean power?[149]

Professor Tinbergen: I do believe that, indeed, we have to be very careful with the present type of nuclear energy. I largely agree with those who underline this. I must confess that I derive my ideas on this subject from a friend of mine who is an engineer, Monsieur R. Gibrat, who was a member of the team that produced the so-called Rio Report.[150] In his opinion, which I found very convincing, we must develop solar energy instead of the present nuclear fission power plants. We also have to develop geothermal energy and, if possible, nuclear fusion energy. This means that for some time we shall have to save as much energy as we can.

D.P.: In a recent discussion I had with Professor Hicks of Oxford he asserted that the attempts made by developing countries to industrialize would face a powerful constraint derived from the scarcity of strategic raw materials. Therefore only a few developing countries will be able to industrialize unless forms of industry that would not be dependent on the traditional raw materials and energy sources could be developed. Now, you have proposed in some of your writings, a world government and a world development plan. Assuming this could be feasible, and if you were to choose an intersectoral strategy of allocation of resources at the world level, would you give priority to industry or to agriculture?

Professor Tinbergen: I think that in a world development plan the

---

148. J. Berger, *Nuclear Power, the Unviable Option*, 1976.
149. J. Tinbergen, *Development Planning*, London, 1967, *Pour une terre vivable*, Bruselas, 1976.
150. RIO—*Reshaping the International Order*, A Report to the Club of Rome coordinated by Jan Tinbergen, New York, 1976.

rates of growth of rich countries would have to decrease and that of the developing countries increase. At the same time a great effort would have to be made to find less dangerous forms of energy, as I said. I would like to add that new technologies would have to be designed that would be adapted to the needs of developing countries. What Fundación Bariloche has studied on these matters is very interesting because this is the first time that a developing continent has, itself, considered the problem that we are now talking about. I think that they should be praised for having made this original attempt. As you know, the limits they see are narrower than the limits Kahn sees. The so-called Rio Report has chosen a position which is intermediate, in the sense that we want the developing countries to develop further than what Mr. Herrera would find possible. However, we also admit that our figures are only illustrative and that their materialization would depend heavily on knowledge that we do not yet have.

D.P.: Coming back to the question of world government, it is interesting to note that a number of physicists and political scientists that met last year at M.I.T. arrived at the conclusion that if a World Government was not implemented soon, the probability of a nuclear war before the year 2000 would be close to 100 percent. The obvious question in this context would be: What would be the basis from which this government would derive its power? I remember an essay written by Bertrand Russell[151] on this subject and he pointed out that the only way to arrive at a solution that would imply a lasting peace for mankind would be to place the control of nuclear weapons in the hands of *a* supranational authority. But it is evident that many countries, especially the big powers, would not be confident in the world nuclear authorities. Therefore this proposal does not seem to be feasible. In this context, when you speak of a world government and a world development plan, what is your proposed procedure to get there?

Professor Tinbergen: I am fully aware, and my collaborators in the Rio Report were as well, that the concept of "world government" may be somewhat confusing in the sense that it would have to be created for a limited number of purposes only. Many people seem to think that I am thinking of replacing all the national governments.

---

151. B. Russell, *Has Man a Future?*, London, 1961.

This is not true at all. National governments will have to continue for a large number of tasks but there are some ten areas in which we need something similar to a world government. Among these ten, the question of arms control and reduction would be one of the most important and most difficult at the same time.[152] All I can say is, I am aware that it entirely depends on whether the Soviet Union and the United States will be able to arrive at a reasonable agreement on limitations of these nuclear arms. The new element in the analysis of this point is the new book by Mrs. A. Myrdal called *The Game of Disarmament*. Her point is, mainly, that it is misleading to think that the power equilibrium that the two world powers are aiming at necessarily implies that they should be of equal strength. If one of the two super powers could have, or already has, the ability to kill a large number of citizens of all countries then there is no need to go beyond that. It is, in fact, craziness to go beyond that. She hopes that this will be a convincing argument for the leading people of the Soviet Union and the United States to stop the arms race. Even if that were to occur, we would still be far from the picture you indicated and the ideas of Mr. Russell. Certainly, at the moment, it is extremely difficult to think of such a degree of agreement between the two super powers. I think this is the most important problem in the world: whether we can reach a state of more confidence between the two main currents of thought. The orthodox communist stance and the other, which could be the standpoint of the mixed society that prevails in a large part of the developed world. So far, it has proven to be extremely difficult for the two to understand each other, but there are beginnings. You have heard, of course, of the institute near Vienna (IIASA, The International Institute of Applied Systems Analysis) where scientists of both groups try to cooperate on several important issues such as energy and the environmental. This is one attempt to gradually understand each other and better trust each other. The other example I could mention is the Pugwash movement where a similar attempt is being made. Both examples show that, even if scientists of the two groups of countries can trust each other, it is not yet certain whether governing bodies will be able to cooperate and limit—that is the point—their own sovereignty on certain matters.

---

152. Arms race, population, food, human settlements, human environment, international monetary and trading systems, natural resources and energy, science and technology, oceans, outer space.

D.P.: Turning to another point that is analyzed in the Rio Report, it seems as though one of the most crucial issues for the establishment of the new international economic order is the one connected with primary commodities in international trade. The lack of balance between industrial production and raw materials is fairly obvious. I would like to present to you some theoretical elements that seem to be relevant. Some authors like Harry Johnson have attacked primary commodity agreements because they think they are restrictive *per se* and because they prevent the operation of the delicate forces of supply and demand that would bring about the much-desired Pareto optimum allocation of resources at the world level. These authors seem to forget that Sraffa challenged the modern theory of value in 1925 when he pointed out that there was a dark spot that disturbed the harmony of the whole. That was the fact that increasing returns to scale were incompatible with perfect competition.[153] The problem of the market structure of many primary commodities (like coffee or oil) is more complicated since there is an additional dark spot. One can no longer assume there is "additivity" of the demand and supply curves, given the spiral of reciprocal expectations of the economic agents involved in the market, when consumers and producers can coordinate their actions (as in the case of the world's coffee and oil market) and traditional theory collapses. Now, you could argue, what about the paths opened by the theories of imperfect competition that were put forward by J. Robinson and Chamberlin? I would be prepared to argue at length that they ignored the main feature of bilateral oligopoly, namely, the fact that every businessman under such a situation, knows that at least some of his rival's decisions depend on his own behavior, and he must take this fact into account in his own decision-making process. Economic agents involved in the markets of primary commodities do not consider that competition consists of a smooth sea (as it is assumed by the Walrasians) where there is no battle because there is never anyone strong enough to disturb his peace. Instead, true competition consists of the life of constant struggle, rival against rival, which one can only find in oligopoly. I think this type of situation is very important, since perfect competition is not generally the case in international trade of primary commodities, but the exception. Consequently, the logical implications Harry Johnson derives from a theoretical framework constructed under

---

153. P. Sraffa, "The law of returns under competitive conditions," *E.J.*, 1926.

the assumptions of perfect competition and perfect foresight are not applicable at all in the case of the world's coffee market or the world's oil market. On the contrary, it is my assertion that when you are faced with a bilateral oligopoly then it is possible to justify a commodity agreement, even at the theoretical level.

Professor Tinbergen: I agree with your statement. I do not agree with Mr. Johnson at all, and I am in favor of UNCTAD's approach. I think that is a quick way of defining one's position. I would also like to add that you were probably right when you said that, in the majority of markets, there is not really free competition at the moment. If you take, for instance, the markets of industrial products then, it is quite clear that the rich countries are protecting themselves against the competition of the developing countries. As you have seen in the Rio Report, we are very critical of this protection. I could also summarize my view in the following way: In principle I see two types of commodities. I see commodities of which the market is stable and other commodities of which the market is unstable. We know important commodities that have highly unstable markets. You mentioned the coffee market, which is very important for your country. It is well known that the reaction time of supply, insofar as price is concerned, is so long that pronounced swings appear in coffee prices. It is a good example of a market that must be regulated, and the same is true for almost all agricultural and raw material markets, and even for some of the industrial markets. These are called the unstable markets and the only way of having an acceptable order here is to have a regulated market. In terms of agricultural markets, the idea of regulations has been accepted, even by such a free-competition-loving country as the United States. You do have, however, a number of cases where the market is reasonably stable, that is, where *disequilibria* can be changed rather quickly into *equilibria*. This is true for a lot of industrial products, but here the great sinners are, once again, the United States and Germany, all of the European community, and perhaps Japan. They protect themselves against the cheap imports with which the developing countries can compete. I think this is a very inequitable situation. We should fully open up the markets of the developed countries for the industrial products of the developing countries.

D.P.: As we all know, there has been a swing in favor of the terms of trade between primary and industrial products. Do you think that the industrial sector will counteract this tendency by raising its prices through a cost-induced inflation of industrial prices? In other words, do you consider that the long-term evolution of the terms of trade runs against primary goods as Prebisch,[154] Singer,[155] Myint[156] and others have pointed out, or would you follow those who took the opposite view: W.A. Lewis,[157] C. Clark[158] and Keynes?[159] Or would Kindleberger be right when he concludes that it is not clear at all at the empirical or the theoretical level that there is a secular movement against primary products?[160]

Professor Tinbergen: I am indeed inclined to follow Kindleberger, but wish to add something to it. We should, quite apart from making a prognosis, try to establish another economic order in which there is more stability and in which the price relations are more satisfactory. Perhaps the most important element in this whole debate is still something different, namely, whether a larger part of the value added to the raw materials can be obtained by the developing countries not by changing prices so much. Instead it could be obtained by changing the division of labor and by establishing in developing countries a larger number of plants which process the raw materials originating from these same countries. I am feeling mostly in favor of this change, that is, that by eliminating import duties we would enable a lot of developing countries to process up to a higher point, even perhaps completely process, their raw materials into finished products. Cocoa into chocolate, textile fabrics into clothing, and so on. This, I think, is the way to get a less inequitable distribution of income between developed and developing countries.

D.P.: I think what you have just said is very important. As a matter of fact, in my country we are trying to develop relevant criteria,

---

154. R. Prebisch, *The Economic Development of Latin America and its Principal Problems*, UN, 1950.
155. H. Singer, "The Distribution of Gains between Investing and Borrowing Countries," *A.E.R.*, May 1950.
156. H. Myint, "The Gains from International Trade and the Backward Countries," *R.E.S.*, 1954.
157. W.A. Lewis, *World Production, Prices and Trade 1870–1950*, The Manchester School, 1952.
158. C. Clark, *The Conditions of Economic Progress*, London, 1957.
159. J.M. Keynes, "Reply to Sir William Beveridge," *E.J.*, December 1923.
160. C. Kindleberger, *The Terms of Trade*, New York, 1956.

which would enable us to have guidelines for an export strategy in the short and the medium term. One of the central issues is to determine the extent to which we can rely on indicators derived from the theory of static comparative advantage, such as the ones generated by effective protection rates and domestic resource cost calculations. It is clear that a conflict arises between the theories of growth and the theory of static comparative advantage if dynamic elements such as economies of scale, external economies and learning by doing, are present. These elements cannot be neglected in an economy such as Colombia's. It is evident that the obvious answer would be a dynamic input-output table. I have serious doubts about the feasibility of constructing one since there is no way to predict the future course of technological progress. Yet I do agree with you when you say that the value added should be increased, perhaps not maximized, since there could be an important trade-off between the increment in value-added and productive efficiency beyond a certain point. The optimum value-added should be given by a well-designed tariff structure, which should be revised periodically in the light of technological process, economies of scale and learning by doing.

Another crucial point is the coordination of our export strategy with that of other developing countries. As you know, many countries are adopting outward-looking policies, and if their strategies are not complementary, a glut of commodities could emerge with the negative effect of increasing the tendency towards protectionism in rich countries. In this context, don't you think that in the establishment of the new international economic order, top priority should be given to this aspect?

Professor Tinbergen: I do agree with most of the things you said. I may, perhaps, add one interesting example that came to my knowledge only recently after we finished the Rio Report. It is a report by the so-called Club of Dakar, a club that deals with the industrialization of Africa. The report is a very interesting document. In particular, I am thinking about the third report, which was discussed in a session at the Ivory Coast. They identified the industries that would be most appropriate for Africa to develop. This is the first attempt of this kind that I have seen. It has been preceded by a somewhat more theoretical study by my friend and former student, B. Herman from Peru, whose dissertation deals with this subject and has been published by the International

Labor Office.[161] The Club of Dakar has used information from many sources including French studies and O.E.C.D. studies. They have applied six criteria that come close to what you have called dynamic comparative advantage. I agree with you that an effort should be made to foresee technological innovations so as to adapt the structure of production in developing countries.

D.P.: As we all know, one of your major contributions to economics has been to the theory of planning. I would like to present to you a few remarks derived from the planning experiences of some of the Latin American countries. Many countries have become skeptical about the usefulness of economic planning, since it is difficult to say that it has been successful given the gap between objectives and reality. How can one explain this situation, taking into account that the technical level of the plans was high? All the traditional tools have been used: input-output tables, Harrod-Domar models, Linear Programming, etc. My own impression is that there has been a considerable distance between plan formulation and plan implementation. I could think of other explanations such as the following:

(a) The rational theory of planning when there is interdependence and uncertainty is in its infancy. There are too many exogenous and unpredictable variables.
(b) The level of aggregation of models like the Harrod-Domar one is too large. Planning of specific projects has been overlooked.

The issue of planning is considered top priority in our institute. One of the main issues of controversy continues to be the traditional debate of the relative efficiency of the invisible hand and the planning instruments for achieving development goals. I do not know to what extent the works of Kantorovich[162] in Russia, and Koopmans[163] at Yale have confirmed your theory of the convergence of economic systems and the theory of the optimum regime.[164]

---

161. B. Hermán, *The Optimal International Division of Labour*, OIT, Geneva, 1975.
162. L.Kantorovich, *The Best Use of Economic Resources*, Moscow, 1958.
163. T. Koopmans, *Activity Analysis of Production and Allocation*, Yale, 1962.
164. J. Tinbergen, *Some Suggestions on a Modern Theory of the Optimum Regime*, Rotterdam, 1960.

Professor Tinbergen: Quite apart from the fact if this forecast of mine is correct, or not, I think we should try to mix elements of both systems. In my opinion, it has been shown that bureaucracy becomes far too elaborate in a country that attempts to plan everything, such as in the Soviet Union. We can also see that countries that try to rely only on the free forces of the market are getting in trouble. The mixed system seems to be the only one that works and, even then, it is a question of having a good mix. Your first question, concerning present day skepticism about planning, I would like to answer in the following way: There is certainly skepticism and, I think, one of the main causes has been a lack of determination on the part of governments to really stick to their plans. This means that the discipline of the governments, themselves, and the efficiency to carry on the plans was not sufficient. Consequently, I am not in favor of inventing more complicated planning methods. I think that you were quite right when you pointed out that in a plan one has to indicate the main features (macro aspects) and then one has to supplement them with common sense and with the invisible hand. All of us are searching for this best equilibrium. If you look at Europe you will see each country has arrived at a different mix, and you can make your own choice looking at the experience of the various countries and, perhaps, find out what has been the successful combination. Even if you are able to make your choice for Europe, it is not at all certain that the same choice will apply to Latin America. After all, Latin America has a different culture from the larger part of Europe, and you may need another mix. It will be important for your countries to act in response to your own experience and try to improve on fields where you feel errors have been made in the past. To learn from one's own errors, and from the errors of others is, I think, the best thing one can recommend.

D.P.: The issue we are discussing is connected with your work on the theory of economic policy. Your celebrated theorem[165] that states that in order to be able to achieve macroeconomic objectives one needs to have at least different economic policy instruments has been, I think, quite influential in the developing and the developed world. Your formulation of the multi-target problem was very important since you showed that its solution depended upon

---

165. J. Tinbergen, *The Theory of Economic Policy*, Amsterdam, 1952.

the simultaneous coordinated use of instruments. Nevertheless, in many countries, governments have not been able to achieve all their objectives simultaneously because important trade-offs exist: between inflation and economic growth, between economic growth and income distribution, between full employment and stabilization policies, etc. Furthermore, some of the instruments selected are not the appropriate ones, given the fact that many times they interfere with each other, and so one gets counteracting effects that disturb the solution of equilibrium. In summary, many countries have applied your theorem concerned with the equality of instruments and targets, but very few have achieved their goals. Could it be that one needs to emphasize the fact that trade-offs exist between policy objectives, and that some instruments do not work effectively in the presence of others, so that one needs to put forward another theorem?

Professor Tinbergen: I think that the analysis you present indicates that it is safer to have a larger number of instruments than targets because then you can maneuver a bit better. Of course, the most recent example that we are facing here, in the developed countries, is this trade-off between unemployment and inflation. I, for one, think that we should attach great importance to employment generation even if that means a bit of inflation. We should also strengthen our anti-inflationary force, which means it is largely a question of convincing public opinion that inflation in the end is unfavorable, especially for the mass of the population, and, therefore it is in their interest to increase the solidarity to combat it. In developing countries the poorest sections of the community are the unemployed and this underlines the need to give the highest priority to employment generation. This brings us back to the problem of designing labor-intensive technologies. In Europe it is important that the strong countries should cooperate more with the weak countries. Germany should follow a somewhat different policy in this respect. At the same time, I agree, remarkably enough, with a recent declaration by Mr. Arthur Burns (President of the Board of the Federal Reserve Board of the United States) with whom I don't often agree. He pointed out that there is a need for all countries to play the rules of the game in connection with the management of their balance of payments. Countries with a surplus should revaluate and countries with a deficit should be more active in keeping their wages under control and similar things.

This requires, of course, a lot of insight to adequately manage the relations with trade unions. At the same time, something has to be offered to them as a compensation for their discipline. In my country, I think that we should look at the higher salaries, which in some cases seem to be too high. We should include in our collective agreements decisions about the highest salaries.

D.P.: We all know that one of your important contributions to econometrics was your pioneering work on statistical testing of business-cycle theories. I would like to take advantage of this opportunity to discuss a few points. I would like to connect the issue of cycles with what we were talking about in relation with primary commodities and, in particular, with the world coffee market. As you know, some authors, like McBean,[166] have put forward the thesis that the idea that foreign trade is quantitatively more important for poor than for rich nations is a myth. On the basis of some calculations made by Coppock, it has been asserted that the un-weighted average for the ratio of trade to income for a large group of underdeveloped countries is smaller in comparison with the corresponding ratio for rich countries. These studies give the impression that there is no clear-cut connection between cyclical fluctuations in the world price of commodities and the internal level of economic activity of the primary producing countries. I am beginning an exercise to show that in the case of the Colombian economy the business cycles one can observe in the last hundred years are closely connected with the cycles we have detected in the world price of coffee. Two of my countrymen have identified, in a rather detailed way, short, medium and long-term cycles taking the historical series of the world's coffee prices by means of spectral analysis[167] and other well-known techniques. It is shown that each cycle is generated by different forces, such as technical conditions of production, the operation of future trading and the relevant meteorological and political variables. We are collecting the relevant data to enable us to associate these cycles with the Colombian business cycles. My intuition is that McBean's thesis, in the sense that instability does not matter, will not apply in the Colombian case.

---

166. A. McBean, *Export Instability and Economic Development*, Allen and Unwin, 1966.
167. R. Serna, "The Dynamics of the World's Coffee Market," unpublished doctoral thesis, 1976; R. Junguito (ed.), *Economía cafetera colombiana*, Bogotá, 1977.

Professor Tinbergen: I am also inclined to disagree with Mr. McBean. The results of the studies you mention seem to be very interesting and their results plausible. It is clear that several forces are at work. Examples in industrial countries also show different causes for a 7–8 year wave and for the so-called American 3–4 year wave. I think that the latter had to do a bit more with agricultural markets although it has never been expressed that way. We have also studies by Ragnar Frisch who tried to analyze various periodicities in economic movements. That sort of study deserves to be encouraged. Certainly it may be of help to dampen the cycles once you have discovered their causes. We must try to make development less uneven in comparison with what it has been in the past.

D.P.: Now that you have mentioned the cycles of the industrial countries, I remember that Schumpeter used to believe in the 55-year Kondratieff cycle whose upswings apparently correspond to major innovations. On the other hand, the so-called Kuznets 16–20 year cycles associated with construction activity seem to have empirical support. Do you believe in the theoretical and empirical support of these long swings in economic activity?

Professor Tinbergen: There have been a number of such cycles but I am not so sure about the Kondratieff explanation. Some people, like the Swedish economist Cassel, thought it is associated mainly with gold discoveries, but others see it connected with the lifetime of heavy equipment. The Kondratieff could be a cycle but also, simply a succession of coincidences. Generally, I think that there are a number of elements that do cause cycles and, consequently, further research would be helpful with a particular addition. The research should be directed as much as possible at finding the instruments to dampen down these fluctuations.

D.P.: Some people have pointed out that the traditional concept of the business cycle is obsolete and that idea has emerged, I suppose, from the observation of almost uninterrupted growth in Western Europe and Japan in the postwar era (with the exception of the last few years). Do you think that the traditional model constructed on the basis of an interaction between the multiplier and the accelerator (Hicks, Samuelson, etc.) would be relevant for the analysis of the present situation?

Professor Tinbergen: Well, certainly less than in previous years. We have learnt a great deal (particularly during the Great Depression) on how to suppress some of the forces at work, but we have been confronted with new problems. So we must have an open mind for new relations and, accordingly, for new policies. I already mentioned that, at present, we are faced with this problem of the trade-off between inflation and unemployment. We did not have this in the past. So, here is an example of the necessity to revise our previous policies and we are in the midst of the debate. We haven't really found a way out, but the principle I want to underline is that to maintain high employment remains an important matter.

D.P.: The question of a high and stable level of employment is obviously connected with the problem of income distribution. I would like to make some remarks on some propositions contained in the book you have published recently on this subject.[168] If I understood well, you have integrated the approaches of the human capital school with that of the school that emphasizes the demand for labor at various levels of education. One of your main conclusions is that the growth rates of education and technological progress are crucial in understanding the forces that generate the pattern of income distribution in Western countries. This is a most interesting point. However, it does not seem to be clear that you can leave out variables such as the degree of monopoly (in the sense of Joan Robinson's imperfect competition), the bargaining powers of different groups, the structure of the tax system and public expenditure, and the relative importance of random elements that might arise when economic agents act in an interdependent and uncertain environment.

Professor Tinbergen: Let me say that I have received quite a few critical reactions on my book, and I agree, this is the way in which science has to make progress. Theories have to be critically analyzed so that we discover shortcomings that enable us to improve our hypothesis. I probably put too much stress on the factors derived from the operation of market forces. I would recognize that the distribution of income is partly determined by what I would call the political will, that is, institutions like social security and similar ones. A large part of the process is connected with market forces.

---

168. J. Tinbergen, *Income Distribution*, Amsterdam, 1975.

A remedy I see to improve the performance of the system is to increase competition in activities that generate too large salaries or profits because they are enjoying a certain degree of monopoly. One way of achieving this result is by means of extending education and to prepare larger numbers of people that are able to manage an enterprise. There is an interesting figure mentioned in *Fortune* magazine (May 1976) where it is stated that the top managers of the largest 500 enterprises in the United States in the year 1975, in relation to other incomes, received 30 percent less in comparison with what they had received in 1952. So it looks as though it is feasible to improve income distribution by strengthening competition for those highly paid jobs.[169]

Now, some of the variables you mention, that have to do with the bargaining powers of different groups were not explicitly included in my analysis. I just received a review of my book that points out that same fact. I think one can develop a framework that could take into account the power of the trade unions and the forces of the market. The action of the former would be reflected in the collective agreement I was speaking of, and the latter would manifest itself by an expansion of business schools.

D.P.: To conclude this short analysis of income distribution I want to make reference to a statement Professor Hicks made a few days ago in a discussion I had with him. He is of the opinion that the international distribution of income is very hard to change since the industrial countries will resist with every resource at their disposal any substantial compression of their standard of living. Would you be more optimistic in this respect?

Professor Tinbergen: I think it is not a question of being optimistic or pessimistic, but of finding the right means to change things in the desired direction. In the Rio Report we recommend the formation of coalitions (a concept taken from game theory and so you may be sympathetic with it). We point out that the organized consumers of Western countries should cooperate more with UNCTAD in order to reduce trade barriers. This is one example where the consumers have not been sufficiently aware of the possibilities of fighting for their own interests. A second example is the coalition

---

169. In the period from 1980 to 2007 top managers around the world received significant increases in salaries and compensation, well above inflation. In 2008–2009 there have been declines due to the world's financial crisis.

that could result between the peasants of the Western countries and the governments of developing countries. Take the policies taken by the United States in the fifties and the sixties. They have paid an amount of money to those who had not used all their land in order to maintain the incomes of the farmers. The incomes of the farmers are of course a function of the price of commodities. It has been shown by the Linnemann Report that, in order to increase the production of food in developing countries, it is necessary to have high and stable prices for food grains. So, you see another example where we could mobilize the agricultural organizations to force the governments into carrying out the decisions of the World Food Conference of 1974.

D.P.: I would like to make a final remark, which is connected with the relevance of economic theory for the analysis of the problems of developing countries. As you know, some people like Myrdal[170] have pointed out that economic theory has been developed with the problems of the advanced countries in mind and thus, it is only the economics of the special case. This position implies, of course, that we should not be too optimistic about the degree of explanatory power of theoretical frameworks constructed in developed countries when applied to developing countries. Do you think this argument is correct?

Professor Tinbergen: I do think it is true, but then we have to specify, of course, which parts of the theory have to be changed. In a way, my repeated emphasis of the search for new technologies is, perhaps, one of the best examples of where we have to change our views. Because, if there is a field where almost everything has been done to the advantage of the developed countries, it is the field of technological research. And here we have a field where we could re-direct research so that we could have industries that are better adapted to the basic needs of developing countries and also to their employment needs. So, in a sense, I agree with Myrdal, but I think we have to be more specific about the changes we should introduce in various economic theories. He did, of course, specify in certain parts of his *Asian Drama*, but I think the question requires more thought and elaboration. On the other hand, we have a rising number of economists from the Third World who have

---

170. G. Myrdal, *Economic Theory and Underdeveloped Regions*, London, 1963.

organized their own institution and who are pursuing the aim of self-reliant research. I am very much in favor of it.

D.P.: In other words, would you say that research about theoretical problems such as re-switching, turnpikes, golden ages and all the elegant theorems of growth theory should be relegated to a secondary position whereas other problems such as choice of techniques and other development problems should have priority?

Professor Tinbergen: That is, perhaps, saying a bit too much. I would not easily dismiss all these parts. I think we have to enquire quite carefully and this, of course, can best be done by the economists of developing countries themselves, because they know their countries better than foreign economists. At the same time they should study the experience of developed countries, since in this way they will be able to avoid mistakes that undoubtedly have been made in our past.

Bibliography

K. Arrow, *Social Choice and Individual Values*, Yale, 1963.
J. Berger, *Nuclear Power, The Unviable Option*, 1976.
C. Clark, *The Conditions of Economic Progress*, London, 1957.
B. Hermán, *The Optimal International Division of Labour*, OIT, Geneva, 1975.
R. Junguito (ed.), *Economía cafetera colombiana*, Bogotá, 1977.
H. Kahn, *The Next 200 Years*, London 1977.
L. Kantorovich, *The Best Use of Economic Resources*, Moscow, 1958.
J.M. Keynes, "Reply to Sir William Beveridge," *E.J.*, December 1923.
———, *Collected Works*, Royal Economic Society, Vol. XIV, 1973. Correspondence between Keynes and Tinbergen and between Keynes and Harrod.
C. Kindleberger, *The Terms of Trade*, New York, 1956.
T. Koopmans, *Activity Analysis of Production and Allocation*, Yale, 1962.
W.A. Lewis, *World Production, Prices and Trade 1870–1950*, The Manchester School, 1952.
H. Linnemann, (ed.), *Model of International Relations in Agriculture*, Amsterdam, 1976.
K. Lorenz, *Evolution and Modification of Behaviour*, Chicago 1965.
———, *On Aggression*, London 1966.
———, *Studies in Animal and Human Behaviour*, London, 1970.
———, *Civilized Man's Eight Deadly Sins*, London, 1974.
———, *Behind the Mirror*, London 1977.
A. McBean, *Export Instability and Economic Development*, Allen and Unwin, 1966.
H. Myint, "The Gains from International Trade and the Backward Countries," *R.E.S.*, 1954.

G. Myrdal, *Economic Theory and Underdeveloped Regions*, London, 1963.

D. Pizano, "A Conversation with Professor Paul A. Samuelson," in this book.

——, "Reseña de libro de Beckermann," *Coyuntura Económica*, Bogotá, October 1975.

R. Prebisch, *The Economic Development of Latin America and its Principal Problems*, UN, 1950.

B. Russell, *Has Man a Future?*, London, 1961.

P.A. Samuelson, "Economic Theory and Mathematics," *A.E.R.*, May 1952.

R. Serna, "The Dynamics of the World's Coffee Market," unpublished doctoral thesis, 1976.

H. Singer, "The Distribution of Gains Between Investing and Borrowing Countries," *A.E.R.*, May 1950.

P. Sraffa, "The Law of Returns Under Competitive Conditions," *E.J.*, 1926.

J. Tinbergen, *An Econometric Approach to Business Cycles Problems*, Paris 1937.

——, *The Theory of Economic Policy*, Amsterdam, 1952.

——, *Some Suggestions on the Theory of the Optimum Regime*, Rotterdam, 1960.

——, *Some Suggestions on a Modern Theory of the Optimum Regime*, Rotterdam, 1960.

——, *Development Planning*, London, 1967.

——, *Income Distribution*, Amsterdam, 1975.

——, *Pour une terre vivable*, Brussels, 1976.

——, (coord.), RIO—*Reshaping the International Order*, A Report to the Club of Rome, New York, 1976.

N. Tinbergen, *The Study of Instinct*, 1969; *Social Behavior in Animals*, London, 1965.

F. Von Hayek, *Philosophy, Politics and Economics*, London, 1965.

www.ingramcontent.com/pod-product-compliance
Lightning Source LLC
Chambersburg PA
CBHW031600110426
42742CB00036B/568